SISTERS IN CRIME
WRITES
OF PASSAGE
ADVENTURES ON THE
WRITER'S JOURNEY

Sisters in Crime
The Writing Life Series

WRITES OF PASSAGE: Adventures on the Writer's Journey
Compiled and Edited by Hank Phillippi Ryan

BREAKING AND ENTERING: The Road to Success
Compiled and Edited by L. C. Hayden

SHAMELESS PROMOTION FOR BRAZEN HUSSIES
Compiled and Edited by Roberta Isleib

SISTERS IN CRIME
WRITES
OF PASSAGE
ADVENTURES ON THE
WRITER'S JOURNEY

EDITED BY
HANK
PHILLIPPI
RYAN

HENERY PRESS

WRITES OF PASSAGE
From the Sisters in Crime The Writing Life Series
Part of the Henery Press Non-Fiction Collection

First Edition
Trade paperback edition | September 2014

Henery Press
www.henerypress.com

ISBN-13: 978-1-941962-19-0

Printed in the United States of America

ACKNOWLEDGMENTS

With much gratitude from Sisters in Crime to those who worked so hard to make *Writes of Passage* such a valuable part of our organization's mission for education:

Beth Wasson, executive director, whose tireless devotion and remarkable skills keep SinC vital, relevant, and important, and who championed this book from the beginning.

The SinC Board of Directors, who allowed this book to be published.

Elaine Will Sparber, administrative/technical editor, who efficiently and painstakingly handled the book's compilation, organization, author liaison, original layout and formatting, and proofreading.

Cathy Pickens, former SinC president and advisor emeritus, who guided the book through its legal process.

Hank Phillippi Ryan (2013 SinC president), who had the idea to create *Writes of Passage*, a timeless collection of sisterly inspiration and shared experiences, and who selected and edited each author, essay, and chapter inspiration.

Kendel Lynn and the staff at Henery Press, who shepherded *Writes of Passage* into this new incarnation.

And all the generous and remarkable Sisters in Crime members who donated their time and skill and incredible talent to make *Writes of Passage* such a treasure.

HOPING

COMMITTING

CONVINCING

ENJOYING

MOVING FORWARD

GIVING BACK

BELONGING

INTRODUCTION

You sit at your computer; the blank screen stares back. The cursor blinks, waiting. The wonderful plot idea you had—where did that go? Why does the whole book-writing thing suddenly seem so impossible?

What's more, you're the only one who feels this way. Everyone else, your mind is certain, is out there typing away, glorious words flowing from their fingers, their book unquestionably destined to hit all of the bestseller lists.

It's only you. *You* are the only one who is utterly doomed to be—

Okay, sisters. Wait a minute.

Here's what I can tell you, the one secret, the one nugget, the one dead-cold certainty of writing: Every single author has felt the way you do. Without question, I can assure you, every single one.

And yet, there they are, smiling at you from their author photos, looking happy and confident and successful.

Oh, yes, the fears are real. The self-doubt is real. So is the second-guessing, and even the lure of the Delete button. Every one of us has faced that, is facing that, will face that.

And that is what this book is about. This little book is your weapon against fear, your ammunition against self-doubt, your antidote for gloom. Are you drowning in indecision? Battling impossible revisions? Have you opened yet another rejection?

Well, if it makes you feel any better, and we think it will, this book is proof that at least you're not the only one. And it's proof that others who have felt exactly the same emotions have come out the other end, smiling from book covers and bookstore posters.

So pick up this book. Open it to any page. The sisters of SinC have shared their journeys—and they have many tales to tell. From Margaret Maron's agent secrets, to Nancy Martin's top ten truths, to Laurie King's search for a mystery family.

And so much more: where to find a place to write, how you know you're a writer, how to start, how to finish, the black moments, how friends made a difference.

We've organized this book the same way your writing life is organized: from the moment you begin thinking about the possibility of a book, to working and then persevering and hoping, all the way through to where, finally, you remember to enjoy it and to give back. They're the "Writes of Passage" every author shares, and these beautifully told experiences can guide us all along the way.

These are gorgeous essays, full of heart and confessions and reality and strength and insight and desire and determination. They are treasures, the deeply sincere experiences of a group of people who are on an individual journey—but a journey we are all on together.

Look for a favorite author. Look for the essays that correspond to where you are on the adventure. Dip in and read any old page.

They say you can only learn from experience. And that may be true. But what they don't tell you is that it doesn't have to be your own experience.

What a joy it has been to compile these. To share these experiences. To receive the benefit of the generosity of these fine authors, and the extraordinary contribution of my fellow editor, Elaine Will Sparber. Thank you, Sisters in Crime, for allowing this project to flourish.

Having a bad writing day? Open this book to any page. You will find a friend, a colleague, a soul mate . . . and a sister.

— Hank Phillippi Ryan

THINKING

"'Poirot,'" I said. 'I have been thinking.'
'An admirable exercise, my friend. Continue it.'"
— Agatha Christie, *Peril at End House*

I GET MY BEST IDEAS
AT YARD SALES

HALLIE EPHRON

Once upon a time, I got a terrific idea. I was at a yard sale at a recently renovated Victorian house. The woman having the yard sale (a complete stranger) asked me if I wanted to go inside the house and have a look around. Of course I did.

I was wandering through the house when the idea came to me. I thought: *Suppose a woman goes to a yard sale. What if somehow she manages to talk her way into the house? And what if she goes inside, and she never comes out?*

I ran home and started writing. The book, *Never Tell a Lie*, ended up being a finalist for the Mary Higgins Clark Award and was made into a movie for the Lifetime Movie Network.

But when I started writing, all I knew was that it begins at a yard sale, and that both the woman having the yard sale and the woman who talks her way into the house are nine months pregnant. The writing went along hummingly (or that's what I recall) until Ivy, my hugely pregnant main character, got trapped in an attic.

Terrific, terrific, terrific, I thought as I roared into writing the book's act III. The stakes couldn't be higher, and there's a built-in ticking clock. Plus I was channeling something scary that I knew intimately: the vulnerability of a woman about to give birth to her first child.

Not so terrific, writing screeched to a halt. I could not for the life of me figure out how to get Ivy out of that attic.

My more experienced writer friends told me, "Just keep writing and it will come." And for weeks I did. I wrote her climbing out the window. I wrote a neighbor hearing her screaming and coming to her aid. I wrote a worried friend coming to the house and hearing her.

It did not come. Too ridiculous. Too easy. Too coincidental. Too predictable. And along the way, I realized she had to save herself.

Six weeks later, I was still stuck. I tried brain-storming. Then I tried skipping over her escape and writing what happens next. Then I tried outlining with colored Post-its. Then I constructed something called a possibility tree. Nothing helped.

Finally I got up from my desk and went to another yard sale. There I was, sifting through a neighbor's old children's games, when I came across Chutes and Ladders. You know how it works. Throw the dice, and if you land on a ladder, you get to jump ahead. Land on a chute and you slide backward.

The answer came to me like a bolt from the blue. I won't say if it was a chute or a ladder that inspired me, just that I had to redesign the attic in order to make it work.

I've now written nine novels, and in every one, I've gotten good and truly stuck at least once. My best ideas for getting unstuck seem to come to me when I'm frying chicken, or taking a shower, or driving, or going to a yard sale. In other words, when I can't write.

So my advice for thinking your way out of a plot hole is this: After you've tried every technique in the book for writing your way out of one, step away from the keyboard.

APPLAUSE FOR THOUGHT

CATRIONA MCPHERSON

Thinking gets a bad press. Feeling's poor relation, action's boring friend, thinking is always apologizing for itself. "Thinking about it" is indecisive; "thinking so" is much less bold than knowing; and God forbid we fall into "overthinking." Of course, "didn't think it through" is another pronouncement often heard, but it's affectionate; there's always a sneaking admiration for the under-thinker—that impetuous scamp. Disdain is reserved for the hesitant, the dithering, the Hamlets.

Even we writers, who think for a living (or hope to), sometimes get squeamish about admitting it. We talk about the Muse; we call ourselves plotters or pantsers; we outline, brainstorm, and mindmap; we happily share our daily word count on our Facebook page, but I've never seen someone post news of six hours' good, hard thinking and expect a high five.

I spent the first thirty-five years of my life being told I think too much. "Dilly Dolly Dreamboat," said Miss Shaughnessy in primary school. "Don't think; write!" said Mr. Pitcairn in high school. "Overanalytical," said my friends. "You could start a fight in an empty room," said my enemies. "You're overreacting/meeting trouble at the gate/jumping to conclusions/just plain bonkers," said a Greek chorus of acquaintances in response to my habit of following every competing notion to every possible conclusion and forming a view of what I found there.

I thought a lot about the consensus that I thought too much. I thought about the alternative and thought it seemed preferable. I thought about what it meant that I couldn't stop thinking.

Then I discovered what it was good for, this high-engagement setting where my mental dial was stuck. I wasn't overreacting after all. I was world-building. I wasn't meeting trouble. I was pre-empting plot problems. I wasn't overthinking what it would be like to be different. I was making up characters who weren't me. And fights in empty rooms? Also known as page-turners.

I had been in training to be a mystery writer since I was five. Who knew?

Ironically enough, I didn't think of that myself. It was my dear friend Louise Kelly who made the connection. I had been writing for a few years and was just about to be published for the first time. Louise had talked me down from some ledge or other and was listening to my remorse. Again. I have no memory of the details, but as I beat myself up for not being my tranquil, placid (did someone say "bovine"?) polar opposite, Louise pointed out that "What if?," "Yeah but what if?," "But what then?," and "Yeah but what next?" were essential stages in the writing of a plotty, twisty, red-herringy, comes-together-in-the-endy crime novel such as the one I had written and just sold.

"I know it's not always comfortable," she said, and followed up with the words I'll never forget. "But that bit of you is where the stories come from."

Those few words changed everything. They set me free. I'll still admit to thinking a lot, a whole lot, even a shedload. But I'll never say I think too much. I'll put my hand up to being very, extremely, or even unbelievably analytical. Guilty as charged. But *over*analytical? Not me.

That's where the stories come from. And nothing would ever make me wish the stories away.

YOU ARE A WRITER

SANDRA PARSHALL

Years of rejection can warp a writer's thinking in dangerous ways and cast a shadow over future success.

Before I was published, I was timid about identifying myself as a writer. A writer is someone who gets published and paid, after all. For years I accepted the loathsome label of "wannabe." After a published author informed me that I was "just a housewife who imagines she can write mysteries," I didn't even feel worthy of the "wannabe" title.

Then my first book was published—by a small press. I discovered that the inner doubts and the disdain of others don't vanish with publication. My book's excellent reviews and award win meant nothing to some people. I was a small press author, not in the same league as those published in New York. I'll admit I let it get to me when a reader told me at a bookstore event that he'd never heard of my publisher (Poisoned Pen Press) and assumed it was a vanity imprint—and refused to believe me when I assured him it was an established and respected press. I was published, but did it count for anything? Was I still a wannabe, not a real writer?

I also heard that if you can't live on your royalties, you're not a professional. Writing is a hobby, something you do in your spare time for pocket change. I was writing constantly, every day, giving my books all my time and energy, and it certainly didn't feel like a hobby, but again I allowed negative thinking and other people's pompous pronouncements to make me feel like less than a real writer.

I've finally come to my senses, admittedly a little late in the day. After six well-received books, I've earned the right to think of myself as a real writer, to announce it proudly and spell it out in the "profession" blanks on registration and application forms. Only the IRS and the state tax department have the right to ask how much I earn—and believe me, they consider me a professional and tax me accordingly.

The wide-open opportunities in today's turbulent publishing world should be celebrated for many reasons, but they don't guarantee best sellers and financial success, the only achievements some people will respect. Writers still have to find a way around the pitfalls of negative thinking.

I wish someone had told me long ago, before I was published, to ditch the "wannabe" label. I was writing seriously, with the goal of publication. I was constantly studying, learning, improving. I was a writer. I should never have let anyone make me believe otherwise. After I was published, I had no excuse for dismissing my own achievements. Books with my name on them, books that other people were paying to read, were the only validation I should have needed.

Often when authors are asked what advice they would give to aspiring writers, they answer: Never give up; keep trying until you break in. Good advice, but I would add: Start thinking of yourself as a writer the moment you decide to devote your life to producing stories for an audience.

You're a writer. That's your identity. Don't let anyone take it away from you.

WORKING

"If you had started doing anything two weeks ago,
by today you would have been two weeks better at it."
— *John Mayer*

"When asked, 'How do you write?'
I invariably answer, 'One word at a time.' "
— *Stephen King*

"In truly good writing no matter how many times you read it you
do not know how it is done. That is because there is a mystery in
all great writing and that mystery does not dissect out.
It continues and it is always valid. Each time you re-read
you see or learn something new."
— *Ernest Hemingway*

JUST ASK SOMEBODY

JOANNA CARL / EVE K. SANDSTROM

I got an email from a reader yesterday. "Dear Ms. Carl," it read. "Hopalong Cassidy wore a black hat."

On page 97 of a book published nearly twenty years ago, I apparently said his hat was white. Her message was polite, but it was plain my error had pained the reader.

Drat! I hate when that happens. I particularly hate it if the reader doesn't believe other things in the book because I made an error.

An accurate background is absolutely vital if a mystery novel is to be believable. I go to great lengths to get things right. And when I get it wrong, somebody like the Hopalong fan tells me about it.

The background details of a mystery novel are the high grass where clues are hidden. Most of the time I am able to get the details right.

How do I do it? I ask somebody.

On one occasion, I needed to know what sort of truck a cattle thief would use. As I was driving past the local GMC dealership, just on a whim I turned in. I intended to pick up a few brochures on trucks.

Naturally, I was greeted at the door by a salesman. I told him I needed to know about trucks.

"What do you want to use a truck for?" he asked.

"Cattle rustling," I said.

I meant to explain, but the salesman replied before I could say anything more. "Then the smallest thing you could use is a half-ton pickup with a fifteen-foot gooseneck trailer."

He didn't demand explanations; he just told me.

This works nearly every time. I've called a glass company to ask what would happen to a storm door if the villain took a shot at someone who was standing behind it. I've talked to locksmiths, hospital administrators, taxidermists, CPAs, the Michigan State Police, and bird watchers—not to mention two or three chocolate experts I keep handy. And I can't remember anybody refusing to give me information. Often, like the truck salesman, they didn't even care why I wanted to know.

I already knew some of these people, but others I hadn't yet met. I just walked in, usually identified myself as a writer, and asked. They were happy to tell me.

The moral is: Everybody knows something, and they love to talk about it.

I spent twenty-five years as a newspaper reporter, and asking questions is what news folks do. But I expected it to be different to ask with the cachet of the local news rag behind me than to ask because I was writing a work of fiction. Early on, I would identify myself as "taking a class in novel writing" to add credibility. But, honestly, it's not necessary. People just love to tell you what they know.

I try to give my sources a free book, plus credit in the acknowledgments, but that doesn't seem to be necessary either. They just want to tell.

I do try to follow a few rules. I do enough research in books or on the Internet to have some background. I usually write my questions down so that I don't waste people's time. If we have mutual acquaintances, I use them as recommendations.

But mainly, I just ask.

Writers, don't be shy! Ask somebody!

WRITING WITH A PARTNER

MADDI DAVIDSON

As a writing duo, we are often asked how we write together, particularly when we are three time zones removed from each other. The short answer is email and Microsoft Word's Track Changes feature. The better question is, how do we mesh differing creative visions without killing one another? As sisters, it hasn't been that hard of a challenge for us, not that it has been all beer and Skittles. (For the record, one of us likes Skittles, the other prefers Coconut M&Ms.) Perhaps we did all our squabbling growing up. Or perhaps it's because writing with a partner is like having a dedicated critique group—one where you get immediate feedback, not to mention someone who will exterminate that pesky paragraph you can't bring yourself to dispatch.

That brings us to Tip #1: You really mustn't fall in love with your own prose. There's no living happily ever after with writing that doesn't advance the story, no matter how clever it is. When your writing resembles a Henry James novel (a character spends nineteen pages wandering around contemplating deep inner thoughts), one's writing partner should immediately wheel it into major surgery. The first time your partner does this, you may feel like your best prose has been consigned to the La Brea Tar Pits and the partnership is *not* going to work. If you need to cry, sulk, or get angry, don't share it with your partner and don't put the excised prose back. (Been there, done that; doesn't help.) Instead, thank your partner for fixing a problem that any good editor would have seen, then get on with the writing.

Tip #2: Writing with a partner is like having one person pass while the other one blocks. You each need to play to your respective strengths. In our case, one of us is the organizer in terms of the plot, outline, structure, and up-and-down lifting of writing. The other one is the "tarter-upper." (That's "tart" as in "adorn or decorate," not "tart" as in "promiscuous," we hasten to add.) The TU adds a turn of phrase, as well as filling in the lines, literally: What does so-and-so look like? What are his or her quirks? Can we get revenge on an ex-boyfriend by naming a dumpy loser of a character after him? (Okay, that last one is not so critical, even if it is delightfully—if a bit maliciously—satisfying.)

Another challenge for writing partners is ensuring that the resulting creation has a single voice. For us, "Maddi" is the writer and nobody should be able to tell where either individual sister started writing. We are lucky that, as sisters, we share the same demented sense of humor, to the point where neither of us can remember who wrote what. Even more telling, when one of us is reviewing/editing/adding to a section, we sometimes find that the other one already had the same idea. However you get there—warp and woof, George and Ira, AC and DC—your work needs to harmonize so that it is one compulsively readable whole.

The best thing about writing with a partner is that it's a blast. That's Tip #3: Pick someone with whom you enjoy writing, as it will make the nine months and/or 75,000 words go by so much easier and "funner." Perhaps the Muse has flown or the demands of everyday life make writing difficult. All writers have these moments. (One of us has had whole weeks of these moments.) The virtue of a good partner is that she becomes the cheerleader, providing reassurance that what you've written is good and if you both just plug away, consistently writing a little each time, you will finish the book. We did. So can you.

Writing with a partner is not really that different from writing by yourself. By yourself, you need a bundle of skills, a bag of tricks, and an inner nitpicker to deliver a truly magnum opus. With a partner, you don't need 100 percent of those skills for every syllable. And you can also have a whole lot more fun getting from "In the beginning" to "and they all lived happily ever after, except the murderer, who got what was coming to him, right between his beady little old eyes."

SENTENCE BY SENTENCE

PATRICIA GUSSIN

Writing a novel is extraordinarily hard work. Many authors enjoy it. I don't. I find any excuse to do something else. With social media and computer games, the reasons to procrastinate have exploded. At least I don't watch much TV. But ultimately, I do get back to the work of writing. And, of course, it's not just the writing, but the self-editing. My first published book, *Shadow of Death*, is "Version M." *M*, being the thirteenth letter in the alphabet, felt auspicious, so in an effort to move forward, I abandoned Versions A through L, lamenting the countless hours of drudgery that they represented.

Version M chosen, I felt a huge relief, until the ping-pong game began. As the manuscript emerged from its cocoon, a slew of agents, editors, friends, relatives, so-called experts, emerged to express their points of view. I was staggered at the diversity of the input I received: make this character tougher, make that *same* character softer, too many plotlines, not enough plotlines, too much sex, not enough, put this scene in, change that scene, take it out altogether.

For a while, I reacted dutifully to this input, jerking Version M around, trying to please everybody, knowing that was impossible, going around in circles. Common sense finally told me to listen to the input, change what made sense, call a halt, and hope for the best.

After final Version M was in play, I attended a propitious writers' meeting. Could have been SinC; I'm not sure. That's when I heard the advice I did not want to hear. After all that work, all those versions, all the ping-ponging, and when I thought I was done, the instructor insisted a writer must do a focused, sentence by sentence analysis. That it was *mandatory* for success. Duh, of course, that sounded like a laudable idea, but to actually go though each and every sentence. Again. How tedious; there were too many sentences among those tens of thousands of words. I was beyond tired of rewrites.

I would assume that most writers know this, that they do this sentence by sentence thing, that it's second nature, but I had not done it. Nor did I think I had it in me to read my manuscript all over. Sentence by sentence.

But I have learned a lot since then, particularly as editor for Oceanview Publishing. I can tell if an author has done the sentence by sentence analysis. It's so clear to me. There are no monstrous awkward sentences; no inappropriate choppy sentences; no prolonged sentences that need to be broken into two. There are no point of view slips. Transitions are smooth, adverbs are purged, words are not repeated too often, lame metaphors and similes are absent, no cutesy tags, and on and on. Well, almost never.

I believe that it's very easy for debut authors to get so absorbed by the story itself, immersed in the critical plot, pace, and character elements, that they may skip that tedious, focused sentence by sentence, grueling review. What I learned was that no matter how weary you are, you need to take that last arduous step to optimize the craft elements that define a pro.

I learned this late in the process, and even though it made so much sense and should have gone without saying, I needed this lecture to force me into the real work of going over the darn thing one more time, sentence by sentence. And then, of course, to read it aloud to make sure it sings.

WABI-SABI WRITING

KYLIE LOGAN

Lately I've found myself doing some pretty eclectic reading. Mysteries, of course, are always at the top of my list. But for reasons I don't quite understand, nonfiction has made an appearance, too. Baseball, honeybees, history. Each topic has entertained and enlightened. One of the other subjects I've been reading about is mindfulness, the active, open attention to the present. Since I've just started my research and my reading, I won't pretend to know what the concept is all about, but I do know it's practiced by Buddhists and I'm pretty sure it has to do with being in the moment. My guess is this might have plenty to do with writing, but I'm holding off making up my mind until I find out more.

As I read about mindfulness, I tripped over another philosophy that does have a direct and pretty obvious correlation to writing. It's called *wabi-sabi*. Again, I don't pretend to understand it fully, but here's what I do know.

Wabi-sabi is a Japanese concept. It's all about the appreciation of imperfection and impermanence. In other words, the acceptance of transience.

As I work to plot my mysteries, I like to remind myself about *wabi-sabi*. My notes don't have to be perfect, I tell myself; they're only notes and not the finished product. As I slap it into some shape that will help guide me through the writing of a book, my outline might have plenty of holes in it, but I refuse to panic. At the outline stage, the holes don't matter nearly as much as the thinking process. Before an outline is finalized, the possibilities in a plot are endless. Half the fun of writing, at least for me, is exploring those possibilities.

Sometimes I forget that. I think because I've come up with a plot point, it's written in stone. I think because one character says thus-and-such to the other, that means those words can't be changed.

I have to remember that a book, at any stage in its writing, is a product that's growing and changing. In other words, it's transient.

With each book I write, I keep *wabi-sabi* in mind. Not every word I write has to be perfect. Neither does every sentence nor every paragraph. Not the first time through. Perfection is an ideal I'll try to achieve before I finish the book and send it to my publisher. But even when I do, I have to remember that an ideal is just . . . well, an ideal. It's not something any of us can ever live up to.

Until then, I'll remind myself that when I'm writing—when the creative juices are flowing and the words are tumbling out of my brain and my fingers are racing across the keyboard—it's okay for my writing to be a little *wabi-sabi*.

JUST CALL ME THE WANDERER

CLARE O'DONOHUE

I'm writing my eighth book. My laptop is where the inventors intended it to be—on my lap. I'm propped up on the couch, pillows behind me, feet on the coffee table, cat sleeping next to me. It gets the job done, but it isn't exactly how I imagined it back when I was just dreaming of being a working mystery writer.

Eight novels into this crazy business, I thought I'd be writing at my isolated cabin in the woods in Michigan's Upper Peninsula, snowed in but with a warm fire and enough groceries to last me until the thaw. Or working at a mahogany desk in my Hemingway-esque Caribbean hideaway, ocean breezes just outside my door. Or, at the very least, typing my next masterpiece in a book-lined, awards-filled home office.

I don't happen to have any writing awards, which is just as well, since I also don't have a home office to put them in. I want one, I crave one, but there's no room at the moment. Apparently, converting a kitchen into an office is considered damaging to resale value. Or so I've been told.

Instead I write at the kitchen table, or on the couch, or—on days when I'm at the "I give up" portion of the book—in bed. As a home-office-less writer, I'm pretty much doomed to wander the earth looking for a place to rest my weary PC, so I'll write anywhere I can find a seat.

Except in public.

I make faces when I write. I mumble to myself. I stare straight ahead in a way that could be construed as odd, even stalker-y, if you happen to be in my sight line. Every writer in the known universe understands that seemingly random facial expressions are really just the author laughing and crying with the characters as they encounter challenges in the novel. Mumbles are dialogue said out loud, to make sure it sounds authentic. And staring—that's thinking. I'm not looking at *you*, freaked-out guy with the half-decaf double latte; I'm staring into the abyss that is, What comes next?

Without an official "writing place," I spent years— years!—working in assorted public places. I thought a coffee shop was the best possible combo of workspace and easy access to caffeine and pastry—a kind of temporary sanctuary for the home-office-challenged writer. But very recently, as I was writing at my usual table, I noticed a woman folding and unfolding the packet of some pseudo sugar she'd poured into her coffee—the kind of sugar that will undoubtedly cause her untold health problems in years to come. As she fidgeted, her eyes nervously darted in my direction, a quiet alarm spreading across her face. Not wanting to cause her fake-sugar stroke to begin any sooner than it had to, I leaned over and explained, "I'm working on my novel," which, as the words came out of my mouth, I realized sounded both pretentious and pathetic. And, I assume by her hasty retreat, not even close to sane.

It's clear to me by now that if you really want to write, you can do it anywhere, but that's hardly the point. In my perfect office—with fireplace, ocean breezes, and awards—the work itself won't get any easier, but at least my facial tics and strange outbursts will alarm no one but the cat. And he thinks I'm crazy anyway.

WHEN WRITING A BOOK STOPS BEING A HOBBY AND BECOMES A REAL JOB

LINDA RODRIGUEZ

When I wrote my first novels (there are several that will never see the light of day again), I had no one, except myself, expecting anything from me. No one really took me seriously. I hardly did. How could I, when writing and publishing a book seemed like such a dream, a castle so far in the sky that I'd likely never reach it. Any deadlines I had for those books were self-imposed. So I could take all the time I needed or wanted to get things right.

Once *Every Last Secret* won the St. Martin's Press/Malice Domestic Best First Traditional Mystery Novel Competition, however, and I signed a contract that included dibs on my next book, things took a dramatically different turn. People, especially my editor, started talking about my next book and about the need to write and publish a book each year. A book a year? I'd taken large parts of over four years to write this book, with lots of massive revisions. How could I write a whole book like this every year?

I sat down at the computer to begin the sequel to my first book and suddenly went blank. That doesn't usually happen to me. I'm the gal who can write anything, anywhere, anytime. But all of a sudden, I felt this immense pressure looming over me. I had an editor and an agent waiting for this book—and, oh, by the way, they expected it to be better than the one I'd spent so many years making as good as I could get it. Cue instant panic and writer's block for the woman who didn't believe in writer's block.

So I called my dear friend Nancy Pickard, one of the first SinC goddesses. Nancy had been in the business of writing these books quite successfully for about thirty years, so I knew she would have answers for me. All I got was her answering machine, however, and I began to have dreadful thoughts that Nancy was on another long tour like the one where she'd covered every library in the state of Kansas. Well, shoot! I'd been sure Nancy would have the answer.

I paced around my house, pulling my hair and talking to myself about disaster and failure, and then I reminded myself I knew how this was done. Butt to the chair. Put words on paper. Any words, no matter how bad, are better than no words. Real writing is always rewriting, and you can't rewrite a blank page. And I sat down and began to type slowly, awkwardly, painfully, until I'd been writing for hours and realized that I'd long since left the awkwardness behind and had written about eight pages.

I can do this, I thought. *I really can.*

At that point, my phone rang. It was Nancy Pickard, returning my phone call after a morning of running errands around town. I was embarrassed, of course. I'd been a panicked fool when I left that message on her phone.

"Oh, Nancy, I'm sorry I bothered you. I was just being silly. I sat down and got started, and stopped having the vapors about it all. I've made a good start, and it's going to work out okay, I think." I know I sounded terribly sheepish, because I felt that way.

Nancy laughed her lovely, silvery, high laugh. "Linda, it's how I feel, how everyone feels, every time they start a new book with that contract clock ticking. You will get used to it."

And I have. It's still daunting when I first begin, but I remind myself that I know how to do this, and I write down those first words, and then more and better words, until another book's done.

HARD WORK
AND WORKING HARD

LORI ROY

My first job out of college was in the accounting field—
specifically, tax accounting. During those early years of my
career, I spent my days combing the pages of the Internal
Revenue Code. I learned how to label and organize work papers
by adhering to a strict numbering and lettering system passed
down from the generations of accountants who came before me.
I wrote with the guide of a ruler, as accountants often do. My
desk overflowed with red pencils, rolls of adding machine tape,
rubber bands, and paper clips. I traded the flip-flops and Levis I
wore in college for blue suits, white shirts, and red silk scarves. I
wore hose, three-inch heels, and double doses of hair spray.
Instead of a purse, I carried a slender brown briefcase, and I
drank coffee from a machine and worked long hours. During tax
season, January through April, I rarely saw the sun, be it rising
or setting. The Internal Revenue Code and the Federal
Accounting Standards Board issued direction, and I and all the
other tax accountants followed.

When, after a number of years, I left the corporate world
and began writing, I approached it as I had my accounting
career. I typed carefully formatted outlines and developed
templates for character studies. I sketched timelines with the

guide of a ruler and tried to identify plot points. With a yellow highlighter, I highlighted books on writing, and I marked important sections with multicolored tabs. On an Excel spreadsheet, I set word count targets and formatted columns to calculate the variance between actual work count and target work count. If I missed my target, the negative result was displayed in a scolding, red font. None of it worked.

While organization served me well as an accountant, it does me no good as a writer. Instead of papers filed in a three-ring binder, the holes of each page reinforced, my research is piled around my office, stuffed in drawers, jammed in manila folders I won't be able to find later. I don't wear suits anymore and sometimes struggle to find two matching shoes as I race out the door. I yearn for the orderly world of an accountant, though I don't yearn to return to that career. I would like a tidier office, and while I accept I'll never be able to write from an outline, I do wish I could, at the very least, write from the beginning to the end.

I began writing when my son was three years old. He's now a sophomore in college and I have finally come to accept there is no labeling system or set of tick marks that will direct me to the next page, no binder that will magically organize my research or my thoughts. My accounting career is behind me, as are the blue suits and silk scarves, but life as a tax accountant did teach me one thing that has carried over to my writing career. It taught me how to work hard. I learned about endurance and deadlines and commitment. I learned to keep at it until the job is done—my favorite advice for a writer hoping to one day succeed.

THE ZEN OF PROCRASTINATION

CLEA SIMON

As a working author, I can attest to one vital truth: There is always time for laundry, and that's not a bad thing.

These days, it seems I am always on deadline. I know this sounds like a humble brag—aka a "diva problem." You know, "Oh, poor me, some publisher wants my next book!" But it is simply my reality and one I share with other writers of serial mysteries. Publishers want series, because series hook readers. And those readers count on their familiar characters appearing at regular intervals. For me, that means three books a year to keep both my current series going. To get there, I write a certain number of words per day, five days a week. Add in proofs to correct, edits and copy edits to address, as well as the freelance reviewing and copy editing I do to bring in some ready cash. It's a busy life.

You would think, therefore, that after doing this for a while, I would have become efficient. One of those people who has a thousand words down by breakfast, leaving time for a brisk walk before settling in with that day's correspondence. That I would have at least conquered the demon procrastination.

Think again. Somehow, as the deadline for each new book approaches, I find myself caught up on the most mundane of household chores—and then belatedly bashing out the prose at eight, nine, or ten o'clock at night. Now that I am finishing what should be my nineteenth book, I am only slightly less panicked about the process (or lack thereof). I am trying instead for a Zen acceptance of my methods. That troublesome subplot will find itself resolved somewhere between the cold and hot water loads. That pesky clue—you know, the one I signified as "She finds clue here" in the first draft?—will undoubtedly come to me once dinner has been started, ideally to be sketched out before I burn the bottom of yet another pan.

I am comforted by the findings of Mason Curry, whose *Daily Rituals: How Artists Work* gives short biographical sketches of a variety of creative types, focusing on their process or lack thereof. (Yes, reading about work counts as work, right?) George Simenon, for example, wrote only a few hours a day and yet managed to produce more than 400 books. Patricia Highsmith spent much of her day caring for snails. Great artists, or even simply highly productive ones, may not be more creative because of their work-avoidance techniques, but they're not hurt by them either.

I suspect I should not be admitting this. I should instead be urging you all to be productive. To apply yourselves. Because I also firmly believe that the ability to write is like a muscle. It becomes stronger with regular use. But if you need time to dillydally, to daydream, or to get the wine stains out of the tablecloth, I say do it. Maybe laundry is part of your process. Maybe those stains are the inspiration you need: the first clue to get you writing.

PROOFREADING:
A MATTER OF LIFE AND DEATH

ELAINE VIETS

I hate typos.

Mysteries sprinkled with misspellings, cozies that use "it's" instead of "its," and thrillers that have "grizzly murders"—beware of those killer bears—make me itch to beat the author with a blunt object.

After I put on my latex gloves.

Typos seem to be getting worse.

I'm speaking as a professional proofreader. I worked my way through college proofreading everything from phone books (snore) to medical journals, including *The Journal of Obstetrics and Gynecology*, along with journals for allergy, surgery, and more. Reading medical journals gave me a lifelong distrust of doctors.

I've never forgotten proofing that stirring editorial in *The American Journal of Surgery* that reminded doctors to count their sponges and surgical instruments before sewing a patient back up.

I proofread from 1968 to 1972 and made $1.59 an hour, $.40 more than the minimum wage. Each medical journal was proofread three times, by three different people. They were nearly flawless.

Publishers can't afford to do that anymore. Now you're lucky if your book is read once. It's your job to catch those typos.

Betty Wilson, a master proofreader, taught me the trade in my hometown of St. Louis. She believed hunting typos was a matter of life and death—and for medical books, she was right.

She discovered that one doctor didn't know the difference between the abbreviations for milliliters (ml.) and millimeters (mm.)—an error that could have fatal consequences. How could a doctor make such a dumb mistake? I wondered. But then I remembered the editorial reminding doctors to count their surgical instruments.

It's harder to proofread your own books. Your mind substitutes the right word for the mistake that's there.

But Betty's three-step method will help you catch more mistakes. If you're like me, you're better at catching typos on paper than on a computer screen, so if you aren't reading page proofs, print out the manuscript.

Here's how I read my page proofs:

1. *Read through the novel once.* Find a quiet spot with good light. Then turn off the TV, CD player, and other distractions, and pour yourself some caffeine. If I'm proofing a 320-page novel, I'll read 70 to 80 pages a day. Take short breaks every two or three chapters. You'll need to stay alert. Pour more caffeine, scratch the cat, stretch, walk the dog, rest your eyes, and then go back to reading.

2. *Finished? Good. Read your book again, holding a piece of plain white paper under each line.* You'll be surprised at how many typos you missed the first time.

When you've finished with the white-paper read, you'll be sure you've caught every single mistake. Boy, are you in for a surprise. It's time for step three.

3. *Read your novel out loud.* You don't need to shout it out. You can mumble quietly in your chair. Your family's used to that. But reading your novel out loud is crucial. Also, crushingly boring. And hard on the throat. So this time, skip the caffeine. It dries out the throat. Drink water. Cold will do, but I use the radio announcer's trick for scratchy throats. I drink hot water with a slice of lemon. It works.

So does reading your book aloud. You will be shocked to find still more typos. I guarantee you'll catch at least four more this way.

Will you get them all? Not this time.

But you will see the last few typos—when your finished novel arrives.

LOOKING

"You must keep sending work out; you must never let a
manuscript do nothing but eat its head off in a drawer.
You send that work out again and again,
while you're working on another one.
If you have talent, you will receive
some measure of success—but only if you persist."

— Isaac Asimov

BREAKING UP IS HARD TO DO

KRISTA DAVIS

Like a lot of writers, I went to the dance with the first agent who would have me. Not the best choice, as it turned out. Two years later, I knew it was time to break up. At that point, I had the strange experience of speaking on the phone with a now-notorious scammer who almost had me believing "no one gets published without a book doctor." He was remarkably convincing, until he offered a great discount if I could send him payment in three days. Hmm, Christmas was only a week away....

Happily, it didn't take long to find another agent. But she had no luck selling three of my manuscripts. Each new manuscript renewed my hope of landing a contract, so when I was ready to pitch number four, I knew it was time to break up again.

This time, I was determined to find an agent who fell within certain parameters. The agent's office had to be within the general New York City area. The agent had to have a sales record in my genre. Preferably, the agent would have industry contacts from having previously worked in publishing. There are great agents who fall outside those parameters. But I had already spent four years with two agents who hadn't been right for me and I was determined that agent three was going to be different.

I did extensive research using the deal search tool at Publishers Marketplace. A handful of agents soon stood out, mostly for their solid sales records. Surprisingly, I received quite a few requests for material, confirming that my research had been on target. Can you believe it? One of the agents was someone I had contacted in my previous search and she remembered that I wrote to tell her I had signed with the other agent two years earlier. Now she wanted to know why I had left that agent. Oof!

Lesson number one: Always break up gracefully and behave like a lady or gentleman. It's a small publishing world and a lot of people know each other. Fortunately, I had a good relationship with the previous agent and had no problem giving the new agent her name and phone number. I doubt she called, but I'm certain my candor about the situation went a long way in assuring her that I wasn't a problem client.

Ultimately she turned down representation of that manuscript and told me why. I could see her point.

Lesson number two: Accept criticism gracefully and don't argue. Agents know their business. This is how they make a living. Whining about an agent's opinion isn't going to win you any brownie points.

I didn't let go, though. I immediately responded with a new idea. We formed a relationship, and about nine months later, I had a contract.

Ultimately, that agent left the business. I don't *think* it was my fault! I was adopted by her partner, who is a terrific agent and a lovely person. It's the best of both worlds. She's someone with whom I would be friends even if she weren't my agent.

If you are in the market for an agent, mind your manners. Don't be public about rejections. They're watching. Don't send a hundred identical queries, because they talk. If an agent isn't working out, it's okay to break up and move on, but break up as nicely as possible. Look for an agent with sales in your subgenre. You don't have to go to the dance with the first agent who happens to kiss you.

"DAMN THE TORPEDOES, FULL SPEED AHEAD!"*

ALICE LOWEECEY

We've all had that black moment. The fifth query rejection in the same day. The email from a beta reader who says she simply couldn't finish the book. The agent who requests chapters and then passes. Even worse: A form rejection on a requested full.

Sometimes, just when we think we've finally—finally!—conquered a level in this game, we pull the "go back three spaces" card. My personal black moment was a two-headed beast. My first agent closed up shop and booted all her clients to the curb. Lots of primal screaming that day. But I'm a stubborn broad. I ferretted out the actual phone numbers of the editors to whom she said she'd subbed my book. And I called them. Their lovely, helpful, sympathetic assistants informed me that my former "agent" had never subbed my book to any of those editors.

That day, I understood what a gut punch feels like. I cried. I yelled. I stopped writing. I stopped talking to other writers. Here I'd thought I had only one more hurdle: getting a publisher to buy my book. Instead it was all a smoldering wreck.

Yet I remembered a similar black moment two years earlier. I'd finished my first-ever book and I was certain it was All That. I entered it in a reputable contest whose entry fee included three critiques. Two months later, my hard copies of the first three chapters came back with abysmal scores. I threw the envelope in the recycle bin.

Then I realized I was throwing away my dreams because I couldn't take criticism. The next morning, I fished the envelope out of the bin. A few days later, I got the courage to open it up again. A few months later, I had a completely revised book, because every single one of those crits was spot-on.

And there I sat. The book could gather dusty pixels on my hard drive forever. Or I could send it—and myself— naked onto the stage and see if someone applauded. Like the day I hung up my phone from the last editor's assistant and realized I had to start all over again. My decision. My dream. My career. Nobody could force me to get back in the race. Only me.

Quit, or damn the torpedoes?

I spread my dreams out in front of me. I'd been writing since age nine. On both those black moment days, I chose not to consign forty years of dreams to a desk drawer. I went out on that stage naked. I started over. In both cases, it was harder than the first time because I knew what I'd almost achieved. I rejoined the online writing community. I started a new book while sending out the first one. I learned how to create better, tighter, more interesting plots and dialogue and characters. Because I control my dream.

One day, I suppose, I should dedicate a book to Admiral Farragut.

*Admiral David Glasgow Farragut, 5 August 1864

LOOKING...FOR AN AGENT

MARGARET MARON

Looking for an agent is like looking for Mr. Right. It's such an intimate relationship that you need to be as cautious as if you were picking a lifetime partner.

A good place to start looking is at the website of the Association of Authors' Representatives (aaronline.org). Although there are many fine agents who do not belong to AAR, you'll be safe with one who does. There are wolves in the lounges and snakes in the grass, but AAR has rigorous standards that an agent must meet to become a member. A reputable agent does not charge a reading fee, an evaluation fee, an editing fee, or a fee of any kind. He makes money *for* you, not *from* you.

Some agents go to writers' conferences and make themselves available for "elevator pitches," a brief and to-the-point description of who you are and what you've written. Think of it as speed dating. Or you can approach them through their websites. While arranged marriages with mail-order brides can work out happily for some, it's best to set up a face-to-face meeting before taking the vows and signing the papers. The AAR site has a list of questions your prospective agent should be willing to answer. Once you've met someone compatible, don't be afraid to ask the hard questions about things that are important to you: How hands-on is he? How quickly can you expect an answer to an email? Will she take your phone calls, or must you go through an assistant?

Most agencies today will require you to sign a clear and fairly simple agreement that spells out the agent's obligations to you, the commission (usually 15 percent on domestic sales and 20 percent on foreign, to be split evenly between the agent and her foreign subagent), and how to dissolve the relationship if it really isn't working—usually thirty days after written notification.

Flirting with a sexy "name" agent can be heady fun, but you want someone who will take your phone calls, who will nurture you, be an advocate for you, pick you up when you fall, listen when you need to vent, and try to help you keep a roof over your head. It is a union not to be entered into lightly because once you commit, getting untangled can be as messy as a divorce: There will have to be a property settlement (contracts and royalties) that could turn into a custody battle over the children (your books).

As one who's celebrated a silver anniversary with the same agent, here's wishing you an equally long and happy ever after!

A LITTLE HELP FROM MY FRIENDS

TERRY SHAMES

The theme song of any writer could be "I'm looking for..."

She's looking for time to write, a place to write, a subject, a character, a plot, authentic details. She's looking for an agent, for a publisher, or for promotional opportunities. She's trying to find readers, and other writers with whom to talk when things are going wrong, or when there's something to celebrate that only another writer can understand.

As a writer, you can do all this looking on your own, reinventing the wheel, gathering mounds of information, organizing it, testing out what works and what doesn't. Or you can go an easier way: ask your sisters. Someone has the information or support that you need and she will willingly share it.

For several years, I was a member of the Guppy Chapter subgroup AgentQuest. It was incredibly valuable for keeping up with the latest information on agents and publishers. But just as valuable was having a group on which I could count for support when I got yet another rejection letter or felt I would never find a publishing home. I still run into people in person that I met online in the group and I feel like I've reconnected with a dear friend.

Last year, I had yet another experience in which sisters played an important part. I was working on a manuscript that had been through many revisions. It had gone out to agents with no takers. I was frustrated and needed help—readers who would give me a fresh read and some constructive criticism.

Suddenly I thought of the writers with whom I was in contact pretty much every day—my sisters in crime. Maybe I could exchange manuscripts with a few writers? I hesitated. It seemed bold to ask for this kind of help.

Finally, I realized I had nothing to lose. Sisters in Crime is a support group as well as an information group, and I needed support. I sent out a general call through the AgentQuest discussion list, describing my book and what I wanted from readers and offering to exchange the favor.

My worry was that I would receive either no replies or too many from which to choose. What I received instead was a handful of thoughtful offers to exchange manuscripts. I sent my work off to four different people and they sent back carefully considered critiques that helped me immeasurably. Two of the readers gave me responses that puzzled me, so I asked for further explanation, and one reader expanded on her comments with such insight that I finally understood what needed to be done. I changed the backstory completely. When I sent the manuscript to my agent, she said, "This is the best thing you've done." And I thought, yes, me—and my sisters.

WHAT ARE YOU LOOKING FOR?

DIANE VALLERE

I'm looking for a sock.

It's a hand-knit pink sock with other colors woven through it. A few years ago, I discovered one in the pair was missing. It's an easy sock to spot due to the bright color and thick texture. Occasionally the one I haven't lost goes through the laundry, and when I'm folding the wash, I get excited. "I've been looking for you!" I open the sock drawer to mate it up, but it turns out I haven't found the lost sock. I still have the sock I knew I had all along. So I keep looking for that darn missing sock.

Being a writer and logging countless hours looking for agents, editors, or readers is a lot like looking for a lost sock. You believe the sock exists, but you don't know where to find it. If you didn't believe, you'd throw the sock you still had in the trash and buy a new pair.

When I first decided I wanted to write, I found myself looking for ideas. Once I had an idea, I looked for plot twists. When I finished the manuscript, I looked for feedback. And once I finished reacting to the feedback, I looked for an agent.

Looking. Looking. Looking.

When I didn't have immediate success, I started looking for my next idea. I kept looking for feedback and agent representation. I looked at less accepted channels.

At the time, I didn't like what I found, so I kept looking. And looking. And looking.

Until one day, I stopped.

I stopped writing. I stopped querying. I put the hard copy of my manuscript on a shelf, much like I left my unmated sock in a drawer.

A year passed, and then two. Then one day, I pulled the manuscript off the shelf and looked at it again, and knew I liked those characters too much to ignore them. So I started the process again, this time looking harder. Not just looking, but listening, too. Listening to the advice of other writers in groups like Sisters in Crime.

And eventually, I went *through* the looking glass and created my own opportunities. I started my own imprint and published two of my series, caught the attention of an editor and agent, and landed a contract for a third series with a legacy publisher. I'm busy and I'm happy.

But have I found what I'm looking for? Only time will tell.

Still haven't found that pink sock, though. Which means I'll keep looking.

CONNECTING

"Authors were shy, unsociable creatures,
atoning for their lack of social aptitude by
inventing their own companions and conversations."
— Agatha Christie, *Mrs. McGinty's Dead*

GROUP POWER, FOR THE WRITER ALONE IN HER ROOM

LESLIE BUDEWITZ

"Only connect," novelist E. M. Forster wrote in *Howard's End*. He was referring to human passion, to our need to belong. But his words apply equally to writing: to connecting with your characters and with other writers. For encouragement, information, inspiration, a reality check. For chocolate, bourbon, or a kick in the patootie.

Writers spend most of our time alone in a small room with people who exist only because we made them up. It's a little crazy and a lot wonderful. But the isolation Forster's character lamented can make us a little crazier.

In 1995, a cluster of new writers—including me—asked SinC for permission to start a chapter. The board debated whether the unpublished had anything to teach each other, but agreed to let us try. An early member dubbed us the "Great Unpublished," and quickly, we became the Guppies. The Internet and email were still fledglings, and we communicated by phone and mail—sharing articles on forensics and publishing, information on agents and contests, and our own ups and downs.

Nearly twenty years later, the information we struggled to find is readily available with a few clicks. The publishing business changes daily, and technology with it. Now the problem is too much information. It flies into your email inbox, gets shared on Facebook and Twitter. You can't possibly sort through it all, let alone use it wisely. Your calendar is jammed with projects, events, to-do lists, and all the other obligations of modern life. You think you couldn't possibly do one more thing.

If that's how your writing life is going, then you need a group more than ever.

I've been reading Susan Cain's *Quiet: The Power of Introverts in a World That Can't Stop Talking* (Crown Books, 2012). Like most writers, I'm an introvert, albeit a noisy one, or maybe an ambivert. Cain contends that most institutions in our culture—schools, corporations, even churches—push extroversion and emphasize group activities and teamwork. That emphasis often results in forming a group to tackle a problem, whether that's really the best solution or not, and discounts key natural strengths of introverts. But while introverts need quiet time—alone in our rooms, with the voices and stories in our heads—we also like to cooperate. We value each group member's voice, and we encourage innovation.

That's what makes the writers' group so powerful. A group can help us learn new information or sift through it. SinC's Guppy Chapter thrives on that principle, with subgroups for those seeking an agent, learning Scrivener, and setting goals. A dozen writers in my neck of the woods recently formed a business and marketing group. The writer experienced with Mail Chimp presented a tutorial for would-be newsletter authors terrified by the specter of yet more technology. Those without Facebook or Twitter accounts met at a café with Wi-Fi and walked through the setup together. I helped the group learn to use our WordPress blog and conduct a blog tour. We teach, puzzle, brainstorm—and toast sales with champagne.

What groups do best, in my ambiverted opinion, is encourage their members and leverage information. Every opportunity and accomplishment I've had as a writer started with something I learned from a group. And with SinC and the Guppies, I didn't even have to put on shoes.

Lawyers—and I am one—often say that a jury of twelve knows everything. Obviously, twelve random folks bring to the table a library's worth of knowledge and experience. But what we really mean is that the process of talking, listening, arguing, teasing out bits of knowledge and experience, and fitting it all together creates something no one in the group knew before.

Come out of your room—metaphorically; no shoes required—and connect.

TRIBE OF WRITERS

SHEILA CONNOLLY

When I started writing, I felt like I had been struck by lightning, like I'd been saving up words for most of my life and they all decided to come out at once. I was between jobs and housesitting in someone else's home, which gave me all the time in the world to spew out those words. So I wrote. I wrote bad books, some of whose names I have blotted out. I wrote series, mostly because I fell in love with my characters and I couldn't let them go. I wrote romance, suspense, and mystery. I wrote light, dark, and anywhere in between. I poured out over a million words before I finally got a grip and asked myself, What do you think you're doing?

And that's when I realized I had to get out of the house and find some people who knew the answer: other writers. I could think of only one published author I actually knew, and luckily, she lived nearby. I called her, and we agreed to meet. After we sat down in a local coffee shop, I said (possibly all in one breath), "I have all these manuscripts, and I guess I'd like to publish something somehow, but I have no idea where to start, and what the heck do I do now?"

She understood. She sent me to the local chapter of Romance Writers of America, where I discovered that I wasn't crazy; that there were other people who heard all these voices in their head, and who woke up in the middle of the night thinking things like, "What if...?" or "She couldn't have done it!" And the biggest surprise? That they were really nice people who were more than willing to share what they'd learned along the way.

I don't know why I expected writers to hoard all their crumbs of information, lest someone come along and grab some of their limelight. Maybe the curmudgeons stayed home, or their books have never been published because they can't possibly show them to anyone else, since that person might steal their ideas or their words. Or maybe the good writers have learned that being nice to clueless beginners pays off in the long run.

I joined Romance Writers of America because it was the first writers' group I heard of, but I didn't stop there, because I learned that I don't have a romance voice. I quickly joined Mystery Writers of America, as well as Sisters in Crime and its Guppy Chapter. And they all shared, too. Finally I'd found my tribe, my clan, my kind of people—the ones who spend a lot of time thinking about how to commit murder.

I went to a women's college, inspired by Mary McCarthy's *The Group*. McCarthy gave me a vision of friendships formed at college that survived beyond those years, and I knew I wanted that. I was lucky because that's what I found at college, and I'm still in touch with many of the people I met and became friends with decades ago.

But I did *not* expect to find another circle of friends this much later in my life, by joining the writers' community. When I started attending conferences, I was intimidated—all these new people, even ones I'd heard of, whose books I'd read, and who all seemed to know each other—and I felt invisible. But that feeling didn't last past the first conference or two. Now I look forward to conferences, not only to learn something about the art and the craft and the business of writing (and to gawk at the superstars, if you really want to know), but also because each conference is a reunion with friends. Many of those friends I "see" on Facebook or in blogs, but it's a special pleasure to get together with them, singly or in groups, and to share what we know, what we've learned, what we're doing, and where we think we're going.

I cannot imagine being a writer without them.

HERD ANIMALS

DEBORAH COONTS

I've heard people say with some authority that writers are introverts. Well, I'm the exception that proves the rule. In fact, one of the great things about immersing myself in a story is that I am surrounded by friends all the time.

At first, this was a great thing, but through the years, I've learned imaginary friends take you just so far. Not only is listening to the voices in your head a bit limiting, it also can be a bit unhealthy. I once had a psychologist friend tell me that to most in his profession, I would be an annuity. My response was something along the lines of, it was so nice to be understood and I would kill him if he chased away my imaginary friends. But I took his admonition to heart. Periodically I emerge from my cave to leave the fictional friends behind and go in search of a dose of the real kind.

Although, after having eschewed the real world to toil away each day in a fictional one, finding "real" friends proved to be unexpectedly problematic. When I would broach a plot problem as the topic of conversation, my friends' eyes would glaze over and they would say, "We can't fathom how you do what you do. We'll read the finished product, but other than that, can we just talk about normal stuff?"

"Normal stuff." Clearly, as a writer, I had a huge disconnect with "normal."

What to do? Well, I limited my happy-hour topics to men,

pop culture, men, music, men, movies, men—you get the drill—and went in search of a new tribe.

But, as we've established, writers are cave-dwelling introverts, and I didn't think it would be as easy as, say, dangling a hunk of meat at the entrance to lure them out—although, if we're talking about romance writers, I've learned that with the appropriate hunk, all is possible.

In the beginning, I was a bit intimidated and flummoxed as to how to reach out to other authors. Desperate, I even considered just walking up to one or two and saying, "Will you be my friend?"

As it turned out, in the writerly world, I had sort of already done that. I had written to be read, and that was my calling card.

Enter Nancy Martin, the wonderful writer of the Blackbird Sisters series and still a true friend despite years of learning my shortcomings.

We met at Bouchercon, the mystery writers' annual wingding. As I pushed through the hotel entrance, this woman rushed up to me, arms open wide, and wrapped me in a bear hug. Yup, Nancy. Turns out she had read my novel (I had only one out at the time), wanted to meet me, and there we were.

Through Nancy, I learned writers really do want to network with other writers—we all take comfort in our mutual affliction. And writers, almost to a one, are the most accepting, supportive, wonderfully weird group of friends I could ever have hoped for.

So, what's the takeaway, you ask? Reach out to the writers you admire. Walk into writers' conferences, groups, and covens knowing that you belong. Grab some wine and join those of us wallowing in our shared idiosyncrasies.

Then reach out a hand to a newbie and bring him or her into the clan. If you do, and if you're like me, you will find friendships to feed your soul. You will find where you belong.

NO LONGER THE ODD GIRL OUT

NAOMI HIRAHARA

Maybe it's because I was an only child for eight years, but I have an issue with loneliness. Whatever divides me from others can feel like a cold knife against my chest. When I was in high school, on Saturdays I used to have to go to a special language school, where I was the odd girl out in a very cliquey environment. I spent most of the recesses in a bathroom stall until I finally befriended another "outside" girl. We would ditch class sometimes and I'd watch her smoke cigarettes outside our Los Angeles campus.

After these experiences, I swore that I would never make anyone feel lesser than. Of course, embarking on a life as a writer may not be easy for those who are plagued with self-doubt. Yet most of us do struggle with perceived limitations of our abilities. After I became a journalist, I was invited to join a women's writing group, and with another member, I organized workshops throughout Southern California. Through this, I began to feel a sense of belonging. Here were others who toiled by themselves in their writing rooms, coming out in the light of day. Most of us, however, had not yet tasted any success of publication. But there was still that hope.

Other than being a fan of Sara Paretsky's novels, I did not know much about Sisters in Crime. The literary novel that I was working on had morphed into a mystery—about fourteen years since I had first started it. I had leafed through the acknowledgments of several different mystery novels to try to identify an appropriate agent. Barbara Neely, author of the Blanche White mystery series featuring a black maid who solves crimes, was a favorite. Even though I had never met Barbara, I wrote to her agent. Within a year, an associate at the agency began representing me.

Now I could faintly feel that my once elusive goal—publication—was within reach. But where could I go to figure out my next step? Who would understand what I was going through? I looked up Sisters in Crime and was so pleased to find that my local chapter, Los Angeles, met at the library in the neighboring town to where I had attended high school. The chapter had, and continues to have, writers read from works-in-progress at its holiday party each December. I signed up to read an excerpt of my novel, which now had a possible publisher. After the event, we readers stood together for a photograph. Other aspiring writers surrounded me, expressing their support.

When the newsletter came out with our photograph, Dale Furutani, a successful mystery writer and Sisters in Crime member, contacted me, offering marketing advice and even saying that he was willing to read my manuscript for a possible blurb. That initial circle of friends continue to be my friends to this day, a decade after that debut novel was published. And Barbara Neely? I still haven't met her but we have exchanged emails.

Today, in my early fifties, I wish I could visit my fifteen-year-old self in that bathroom stall and whisper in her ear, "Someday you'll find a place where you belong."

FINDING MY TRIBE

LIZ MUGAVERO

Since I was a kid who always had plenty of friends, my parents thought it odd when I said I never felt like I fit in.

"But why?" my mother would ask. "You're always with a group of people. Someone's always calling the house. I don't understand."

She was right. Most people liked me. I could easily adapt to different groups and get along with all of them—the popular kids, the geeks, the in-betweens. Growing up, I had the same posters of Johnny Depp as the other kids in my class. The difference was, right next to Johnny was a poster of Freddy Krueger.

None of the other kids in my class had that.

There were very few who "got" me. In retrospect, I didn't quite get me either, so it wasn't a surprise. There weren't many people with whom I could have real, meaty conversations. When I could, the topic was usually books, authors, or crime. But I hadn't yet found many people who shared my interests, so I spent most of my time reading. Usually about crime.

I felt a real kinship in college with a professor who could analyze Poe like no one I'd ever met. Who made me feel it was acceptable to spend time poring over literature looking for meaning, to find joy in the written word. To write entire papers on the macabre.

In grad school, it was even better. I was finally around other fiction writers. People who wanted as badly as I did to write books and put their words out in the world. I had a lot of meaningful moments in those classrooms. I wrote a lot of pieces and validated my talent. I got my first short story published. I sold an essay I'd written during a class exercise. I wrote an entire novel for my thesis.

After school, I floundered again. Took up journalism—didn't get the crime beat—and dreamed of writing books full time. One day it hit me. I loved to read mysteries. Why wasn't I writing them?

So I started doing that, with no good idea what I was doing.

Then I found a little conference called Crime Bake. Perusing the website, I could barely contain myself. Mystery authors, forensic experts, police, FBI agents. I knew I had to be there.

That first year I attended, nearly ten years ago, I had a fellow crime-writing friend with me. We knew no one but were giddy with excitement at simply being among so many writers, surrounded by books. We attended every panel and took copious notes. We had books signed by "famous" authors. We imagined sitting on a panel ourselves one day.

At cocktail hour, a man approached us. We recognized him from around the conference; he was clearly part of the "in" crowd. After finding out it was our first Crime Bake, his eyes lit up. "Oh, we're so thrilled you found us," he said. "Mystery writers are the best group to belong to."

That man was Al Blanchard, a driving force behind the Crime Bake conferences. The community lost Al shortly thereafter. I'd known him for only a half hour, but I know his message did not find me accidentally. He was telling me I'd found my tribe. I was finally home.

I love being part of the mystery community. Why wouldn't I? They all get me.

HOPING

"Do not spoil what you have by desiring what you have not;
remember that what you now have
was once among the things you only hoped for."
— *Epicurus*

"'Hope' is the thing with feathers—
That perches in the soul—
And sings the tune without words—
And never stops—at all—"
— *Emily Dickinson*

HOPING FOR THE BEST: A CAUTIONARY TALE

SUSAN M. BOYER

It seems that hope is a necessary pharmaceutical in every phase of a writer's journey. In the beginning, I sipped hope and prayed I could complete a book. I poured bigger cups of hope as I wrestled the first book into something someone somewhere would want to publish. I learned so much during these years—yes, years. Workshops, conferences, critiques, craft books, et cetera. But there was a freedom as well, because in the beginning, I was hoping for things I had some degree of control over. I could work harder and drink deeper from the well of hope.

The next leg of the trip, querying agents and publishers, required a stronger glass of hope, something more akin to daily Jell-O shots of faith. Too many things were simply out of my control, and I'm a control freak. The thing I discovered during this roller-coaster ride is that hope is not always my BFF. You have to keep an eye on hope or she will lead you down the wrong path.

The first time an agent asked for a revise and resubmit, I was thrilled. She was so encouraging and genuinely excited about my manuscript. But she just needed me to rewrite it in third person and take out a dozen characters, and maybe someone else could be the killer?

Here is where hope got me into trouble. I wanted an agent so badly, had hoped for one for so long, that I ignored the small voice inside insisting these changes were not right for my story. If I could just get my foot in the door. . . . I spent six weeks on those revisions. When I sent them in, I was starry-eyed and filled to the brim with hope. Despite repeated attempts to contact this agent, I never heard from her again.

When the next agent asked for completely different revisions, I was grateful I'd saved my original manuscript. I guzzled hope as I worked for two months to make my manuscript everything she wanted. But when I finished, she didn't have time to take a look.

Apparently I'm a slow learner. I went through several more rounds of revise and resubmit, each time hoping to turn my manuscript into a different agent's completely different vision of what would sell. I did manage to ignore the request to add vampires or possibly pirates—not that I have anything against either. They just didn't belong in my manuscript. Eventually, I grew to love the words that had once pushed me to threaten to set my hair on fire: "It's just not right for me." Finally, I understood the level of subjectivity in publishing.

At the end of the day, we're all readers, right? Authors, agents, editors—we are all readers first. But not everyone loves the same books. And even if a reader loves a book, it might not be the kind of book needed on any given day for any given publisher's list. Hope will not change the publisher's list, and if you revise a manuscript too many times, you could end up with a Frankensteinian mess. I did.

However, two positive things also came from this experience: first, all that rewriting surely made me a better writer, and second, it sent me running to an excellent freelance editor. I was so confused by all the conflicting directions that I needed someone to point me down the right path. She asked questions that made me think, offered keen observations, but never once told me what to write or how to write it.

Ultimately, I found a publisher and later an agent who shared my vision for my work. Of course, there were still edits to be done. Everyone needs an editor, and I adore mine, even when I'm curled in a fetal position in the closet wailing over a red-line edit. But I wish I had back all the time I spent trying to make my manuscript something it wasn't based on hope. Because I now need every drop of that hope for the next phase of my journey.

WISHIN' AND HOPIN'

KAYE GEORGE

Do you remember the song by Dusty Springfield? "Wishin' and hopin' and thinkin' and prayin'"? She concluded, in the song, those wouldn't get her into his arms. I found out they wouldn't get me into print either. Still, when one is writing and trying for publication, one can't help but hope! In fact, you have to.

I loved my Sisters in Crime group in Dallas. When we moved way far out of Dallas, to a tiny town near Wichita Falls, Texas, for my husband's job, I was bereft without my fellow crime lovers.

My husband and I had made a deal for his new job. With this move, I would quit computer programming and write full time. That had always been my dream. I would polish my novel and get it published. I loved programming but had been working contract jobs and they were getting more and more scarce after Y2K. If you don't remember that term, it's what we called the year 2000. Some people feared that event would wreak havoc among computer codes throughout the banking and insurance industries. Maybe some others, too, but those were the ones on which I worked. I felt super good about the work my team did on our many assignments, but we had been well paid. Too well paid. After Y2K, no one wanted to pay much, or even hire many programmers, for regular work.

So off we went to tiny Holliday, Texas, and I settled in to writing full time. And hoping to get published. I bought Jeff Herman's latest guide and pored through it, noting every agent associated with mysteries. Then I started querying them. I know what you're thinking: Good luck with that. And you're right. I had no luck at all.

There were also no mystery writers in the area, or none that I could find. I located some romance writers. A very friendly bunch, but they weren't a bit interested in weapons or poisons or forensics, or even in killing people. It was a lifesaver when I found the online SinC Guppy Chapter.

I began to get the discussion list and avidly read and absorbed everything I could. I learned how to write a good query letter and, just as important, how to query—not too many at a time. I learned how to treat point of view. How to introduce a scene. How to structure a mystery. How to use dialogue.

But I think the most important thing I learned was that this is not an easy process and it would take time and patience and tons of persistence. I learned of writers who wrote seventeen books before getting one published. And writers who tried for fourteen years before it happened.

Well, by golly, if persistence was what it took, I'd give it persistence. After nearly 200 queries on the first one, I wrote another and queried it. Then I wrote another and queried it. Then I wrote another—and got it published. From the examples I had, I never gave up hope. I knew it would happen one day.

Someone told me of the Magic Number Theory. I embraced it and have repeated it often. Every querying writer has a magic number. If your number is 18, you'll get published after 18 queries. If it's 235, you'll get published after that many. You don't know what your number is; you just know that each rejection gets you closer to your magic number. That little theory gave me the hope I needed to keep on and on and on. My magic number was 468.

BEING HOPEFUL
REQUIRES STAMINA

DARYL WOOD GERBER / AVERY AAMES

Are you ready to give up? Don't!

It's not easy getting published. It's even harder to remain hopeful while on the journey. Staying positive takes tenacity. Belief in yourself requires passion. And above all, you need friends who won't let you flounder.

I started out as an actress (lots of rejection; lots of success), but then I moved out of Los Angeles and that dream ended. However, during my stint in Hollywood, I wrote a number of screenplays and television shows, so when I left the business, I considered myself a writer. A writer can write anywhere.

Over the next fifteen years, I penned a number of books, both traditional mysteries and suspense. I submitted these books to agent after agent and received comments like, "I love your writing. This is so close, but it's just not for me. What else do you have?" What kept me going? Remaining hopeful. Believing I *could.*

About five years into that fifteen, I joined a Sisters in Crime chapter in Charlotte, North Carolina, as well as the SinC online Guppy Chapter. I listened to what other members told me, and I offered my cheerleading expertise in return. I'm a great cheerleader. I know how to set goals and grind away until I achieve them.

However, even with the positive input and the rah-rah mentality of never giving up, after a few more years of agents writing, "No, not for me. Got anything else?" I was ready to throw in the towel. I had submitted my last thriller to agents. If that didn't wow them, well, I was going to quit.

Luckily, a beloved critique partner suggested I try one more book and write to the market. "Cozy mysteries are selling," she said. To date, my mysteries were bordering on hard-boiled. Before following her advice and knocking out another 300-plus pages, I needed to do some research. I read a number of cozies and I studied the style. Also, I wanted to make sure that the cozy hook I chose was a good one. You see, a hook matters in the cozy world. It's like branding or name recognition in other fields. So I approached an agent I had met at a number of conferences, most recently at New England Crime Bake. She was actually the agent for a number of Guppy authors and also had given me encouragement on previous work. I asked her if I could submit cozy ideas to her to see if they would fly with a publisher. She agreed. I submitted professionally crafted bibles that included three sample chapters, an overview of the series, character sketches, and a basic outline, but none captured her fancy. I received high praise from her, but none of the ideas was *just right*. By the end of the exercise, my frustration was at an all-time high.

Ultimately, I returned to what I had been writing before I changed track—a thriller. I dusted it off, polished it, and continued the quest to find an agent who would think my thriller was the most brilliant piece of writing ever. I received requests for full manuscripts and was feeling pretty sure that something would break for me this time...soon. However, within weeks, I was once again of the mind to quit. Q-U-I-T! Period. End of story.

Then one day, out of the blue, I received an email from the agent who had been helping me come up with a cozy mystery hook. She asked if I would be interested in writing A Cheese Shop Mystery series. Writing about a cheese shop sounded like tasty fun. I loved to cook. I used to cater. And per the series bible, the grandmother who raised the protagonist was a sassy character who managed the local theater. This was a perfect fit. Long story short, the publisher loved my sample chapters and I got the job. I was going to be published, writing something I truly enjoyed!

Sticking with the game of publishing long enough to get published takes hope. If you believe in yourself, continue to hope. If you have fingers that can still type and ideas that still brew in your mind, continue to hope. If you don't, look for friends who will reassure you. And when opportunity knocks on your door, open it and say, C'mon in.

Are you ready to quit? Don't!

HOPE SPRINGS ETERNAL

JENNY MILCHMAN

Hope filled my days for the eleven long years I spent trying to get published. Hope the color of candy; hope as fragile as dandelion spores.

During those eleven years, I wrote eight novels, five of which were submitted by three agents and received fifteen almost-offers. Why "almost"? Well, after an agent interests an editor, the editor has to get approval from the rest of the house. And if you think about how variable opinions can be about a book—just join a book club—then you get an idea of how difficult it can be to sell one.

It's hard to live on the cusp of something for more than a decade. Back when I began writing and querying and going on submission, my husband and I were at that age when hopeful grandparents start worrying about falling fertility rates and whether they will still be young enough to get down on the floor when the grandchildren finally do come along.

"Should we start trying?" I would say to my husband.

"But you're going to be published any day now," he would reply. "And then, who will have time for a baby?"

Those babies were in first and third grades by the time my first book appeared.

In between believing it was just about to happen and learning the ropes of this business and how deeply you have to dig in order to write publishable fiction, there were an awful lot of dark nights. And tears. And me saying, "I can't do this anymore," to the aforementioned husband.

So where did the hope come in?

I was the proverbial donkey with a carrot during those eleven years. There was always a chance dangled just a few feet in front of me. There was always something to *hope* for.

An agent who'd asked to see pages, an editor who would take my book to editorial if I made a few changes, a new novel to write. I kept myself in the game by always reaching for that carrot.

When you're on submission, you do a lot of waiting around. Thomas Edison said, "Everything comes to him who hustles while he waits." At a certain point, it hit me that the linear path of agent–submission–book deal might not be the one for which I was destined, and so, while I was waiting, I also started hustling. I went to book signings, joined writers' organizations, and attended conferences.

My eighth novel had been turned down everywhere, getting so close that my final rejection came from the publisher of the house herself.

But by now, I had become part of a community of authors and writers and readers.

And in the end, one dear and special member stepped in.

One of my favorite authors, Nancy Pickard, was kind enough to read the unpublished manuscript that everyone had turned down. And to put it in her own editor's hands.

You might expect that when I heard this, I starting hopping around, hugging myself, and counting chickens. Except that you're reading this, so you know better.

"That is just amazing," I thought. "What a thing for her to do. If we were having any more children, I would name them all

Nancy. But I've walked this block a time or two or fifteen. I just can't keep hoping."

Except maybe I did hope, a hidden little bit.

And then Nancy Pickard's editor bought my book.

It never would've happened without the community for which this very piece is being written. It never would've happened if I hadn't kept trying.

It never would've happened without hope.

TOO MUCH HOPE

BARBARA ROSS

It is possible to have too much hope.

Let me explain. For years, I made my living as an entrepreneur and routinely pitched venture capitalists, investment bankers, and "high net worth" individuals looking for money. If they "didn't get" my business plan or the deal wasn't in their sweet spot, I walked away thinking, *Their loss.*

But when, on its lo-o-ong road to publication, my first book was rejected by agents and then by publishers, I was emotionally devastated. I just did not understand why I couldn't shrug it off.

I asked my writer friends. Everyone had felt the phenomenon, but no one had an answer. "It's because a book is so much more personal" was the most common explanation. But I didn't fully buy it. When you've put your time and your brain and your heart into growing a business, and especially when you've involved colleagues whom you respect and even love, believe me, it's personal.

Here's what I finally concluded. You bled and sweated to finish that first manuscript. You stole time from your family and your job, and sometimes that swamped you with guilt. It was harder to write your book than you ever imagined. And you're not sure, given all you went through, if you'll ever be able to finish another book, much less a good one.

Now you're sending your book out into the world freighted

with all your hopes and dreams. If you've always wanted to be a writer, your book may be carrying your very identity, your self-worth, and your self-confidence on its slim back.

It's too much hope. It's like a dozen elephants standing on a slender pin. It becomes too easy for hope's parasitic twin, fear, to take over. And then, even though you have hope, you're afraid to look in your mailbox, afraid to open that email. Your stomach churns when the phone rings.

My first book, *The Death of an Ambitious Woman*, quickly garnered interest from multiple agents. I signed with one, and then the book didn't sell to a publisher. As the weeks and months rolled by, I had hope, but I also had fear. And when my agent told me we were done, I fell down the rabbit hole. I was crushed. If I'm honest with myself, I have to say that rejection set me back years.

The most important character trait a writer can have is not hope. It's resilience. But how do you get it?

You write more. I know it's what everybody tells you to do, but it works. Because it takes the pressure off that first little book. Your book doesn't have to carry the full burden of your dreams. The load can be shared with a second book, and maybe a third, and some short stories if you're so inclined. "There are always more words," a member of my writers' group used to say while cutting great swaths out of her manuscripts.

There are always more words. There are always more characters. There are always more stories. There are always more books.

Embrace it, believe it, and, most importantly, practice it, until it takes you to a place where, when an agent or publisher "doesn't get" your book, or says they love it but don't know how to sell it, you reflexively think, *Your loss*, and go on your merry way, until you finally find a match.

THE HOPE CHEST

SHARON WILDWIND

Once I had a child's prayer book with ribbon bookmarks and three silver charms: a cross (faith), a heart (charity), and an anchor (hope). I thought hope was something that kept me always tied to the same place. Years later, one sentence led me to understand hope in a new way.

"Hope is the ability to imagine a tomorrow that we find enjoyable and life-giving and to know that we have the resources to achieve that preferred future." (Dr. Robert J. Voyle, psychologist and minister)

My knee-jerk reaction equates resources with money. If that were true, I'd see a hopeless future. Writing will never make me rich. Fortunately, resources are a lot more than money.

Resources are like library books: we borrow them for a while. If I belong to a great critique group, my task is to enjoy the group and make a contribution, not worry that someday, it will break up. If writing engages me, my job is to write, not fret whether I'll ever have another great idea.

Hope helps me express what I need as positive outcomes rather than settle for negative ones. If I hope for fewer problems with someone and get this, I'll still have problems with that person. If I hope to build a working collaboration with that person, I'll create a new ball game.

The writer's life is a marathon. There came a time I hunkered down, hoping only to survive. By concentrating on survival, I lost the connection to doing what I loved. If I wanted to go the distance—and I did—I had to create a hope chest and keep it filled.

This is not easy. In Pilates, I learned to strengthen my core muscles. For my hope chest, I had to learn to keep my emotional core strong. My heart's core is one sentence: I am a writer. That's my absolute fallback position. When the world unravels, I drop back to that truth. I am a writer.

Sylvia Boorstein, a Zen teacher, author, and psychotherapist, has the perfect self-talk for tough times: "Sweetheart, you are in pain. Relax. Take a breath. Let's pay attention to what's happening. Then we'll figure out what to do."

When I say that to myself, the negative thoughts stop. After I have relaxed, breathed, and paid attention, I try to come up with at least three positive statements. The first one is often, "I am a writer." I wish I could say the rest were, "I've succeeded in tough situations before. I have resources, including people rooting for me. I will cope."

It's more likely to be, "I'm furious. The world stinks, and I am surrounded by idiots," followed by binge DVD watching, making art, or taking a long nap. Don't kid yourself. Those occasional excesses fill the hope chest, too. Sometimes taking time off gives me the thing I most need—perspective.

Taking care of my body fills the hope chest big-time.

In a perfect world, I'd exercise every day. Daily exercise is important because muscles are chemical factories. Exercise opens those factories for business. The chemicals produced promote positive feelings. The more positive I feel, the more hope I have.

Months ago, I converted to a standing desk. My productivity shot up and stayed up. Check out on the Internet why sitting more than twenty minutes causes blood vessel damage, and how standing and treadmill desks can prevent this. If you can't see a standing or treadmill desk in your future, at least stand up every twenty minutes.

Want to add a quick fix to the hope chest? Drink water. Two percent dehydration, an amount too small to trigger thirst, impairs decision making and reduces creativity. Sometimes hope is as simple as a glass of water.

In the words of *Galaxy Quest*'s Jason Nesmith, "Never give up. Never surrender." That's what hope is all about.

COMMITTING

"Choose a job you love,
and you will never have to work a day in your life."
— *Confucius*

"The secret of getting ahead is getting started."
— *Agatha Christie*

"Your purpose in life is to find your purpose
and give your whole heart and soul to it."
— *Gautama Buddha*

THE DAY I BECAME AN AUTHOR

JOELLE CHARBONNEAU

When I started writing, I wasn't a mom, which meant I had lots of time to dedicate to things that I liked. Writing was a hobby, and I found it relatively easy to fit the fun of creating a story in between work and family. Then my son was born and everything changed. I thought I understood what other writers meant when they talked about life intrusions, but until I lived it, I had no idea. Suddenly, writing wasn't an interesting adventure I explored in my free time. Because there was no free time. If I wanted to really improve and grow as a writer, I would have to commit to making the time. And doing that . . . well, it was work.

There were days I was too tired to write. There were days I wanted nothing more than to curl up with someone else's story and lose myself in the wonder of books that made me want to write in the first place. But as much as I wanted those calm moments where I didn't have to think, let alone work, I didn't give in to them. Because I had made a commitment to myself to become a better writer. Not to be published, although had the opportunity presented itself, I certainly wouldn't have turned it down. But what I wanted most was to walk the path that would lead to being the best writer I could be. And to do that, I had to write. Not just when I wanted to, but every day, no matter how tired or excited or sad or distracted I was.

Making the commitment to sit in front of my computer and write, not because of a deadline or a hope for monetary gain, was the best choice I have ever made. Because while the business of writing and the hope of publication were in the back of my head, it was the story and the quest to tell it to the best of my ability that drove me. I learned to self-motivate based on love of the craft and the thrill of climbing the storytelling mountain and getting to the other side.

Since that time, I have become an author. Not because I have books in bookstores, although I do. And not because readers who aren't my family have read my stories, although they have. Those things are wonderful, and I am incredibly thankful for both the publishers and readers who have allowed me to make writing my full-time job, but they are not what make me an author. I didn't realize it at the time but I became an author long before the day I got "the call" or held my first book in my hand. I became an author the day I made the commitment to myself and the story I was telling. I became an author the moment I chose to make the telling of the story a priority. I wish I had noted that date down on my calendar, because every year, I would celebrate it as one of the most important days of my life.

MAKING THE COMMITMENT

MEREDITH COLE

It is very easy to begin a book. I can type "Chapter One" and an exciting first sentence in less than a minute. I can sit back and dream up exciting characters and new plot twists for hours at a time. When a book is still new, there is nothing in it that I have to fix. It just contains endless possibilities. Finishing the book is another matter. Committing to a book and seeing it through to the end is much harder, and it is why there are so many beginnings of novels sitting in drawers and hard drives around the world.

When I began my first novel, I was pregnant with my son. I had decided that I did not want to work in TV forever, and that it would be difficult to continue to make independent films on a shoestring once the baby arrived. I wanted to tell stories, and I started my first mystery on a dare from a friend. I loved to read more than I liked to watch TV or see movies. It seemed silly not to write novels. So I began a novel as a fun side project.

Along the way, the book became less fun. It became work. I could see it was not as good as books I had read and admired, and I wanted to make it better. I had been a writer for years, but I had written essays, screenplays, letters, and advertisements. Writing a novel felt a little like learning a new language.

I put the book down for a couple of months. I tried again.

And then I realized that I needed to get serious if I was ever going to become a published writer. When I was named a playwriting/screenwriting fellow by the New York Foundation for the Arts, I used some of the money to join the Writers Room, a shared work space for writers in Manhattan. I made a commitment to go regularly to my new "office." I joined Sisters in Crime and Mystery Writers of America and found a community of other writers. I said, "I am writing a mystery" out loud, and the book became more and more real to me.

Through Sisters in Crime I also found a small writers' group. Two of the women in the group were published mystery authors. We made a commitment to each other to meet every other week. The women took my first efforts seriously and told me what they liked and what didn't work in the pages I shared with them.

I went back to the book I had worked on for so long and saw clearly for the first time everything that was wrong with it. And I put the book aside and started anew. I took what had worked from my first efforts—the setting and interesting characters—and created a story where the stakes were higher for my protagonist. I knew the characters well, so that second book was easier and faster for me to write. Struggling through my first effort had taught me valuable lessons and skills. I now wrote regularly. I was committed to turning in pages to my writing group. I was committed to making my second book good. And I gave myself a deadline for finishing.

In less than a year, my second book became *Posed for Murder* and won the St. Martin's Press/Malice Domestic Best First Traditional Mystery Novel Competition. And I was proud to discover that I had become both a professional author and a writer committed to my craft.

THE SHOW MUST GO ON

SUJATA MASSEY

Writing careers are erratic. Even the most hard-working, committed author may run into long stretches of time when no new book is coming out.

I had a long dry spell between my tenth mystery-series novel and my first historical novel. The research, writing, and selling of my spec book took about five years. And from the point my agent found an editor willing to buy the book, it took eighteen more months for the contract, editing, and production of the book!

Over this time span—six and a half years—quite naturally I was not receiving invitations to sign at bookstores, lecture at libraries, or participate in literary festivals. I stayed away from mystery conventions because I didn't want to spend hundreds of dollars going somewhere when I had no new book to be signed. And while I was working very hard writing on the laptop on my dining table, being out of the public world caused feelings of isolation to build up within me.

It was only when my new book came out that a whirlwind of activities came my way. Once again, I found myself in all kinds of venues, meeting readers and having wonderful conversations. Because I felt like a working member of society, my mood zipped upward. It was easier for me to meet daily writing goals and organize my schedule.

I would have been happier and more productive during the quiet years if I'd had public engagement. And I've belatedly come to understand that you don't necessarily need a new novel out each year to participate in the book world. Unless you are one of the few who absolutely hate signings and book promotion, you need to be with people. You must ensure that you don't get so lonely and discouraged that you give up your writing.

Here are a few things that any previously published writer could do for herself between books.

- *Moderate a bookstore event.* Audiences love to see one author interviewing another. It makes them feel like they're eavesdropping. It's especially great if you're interviewing a writer friend or someone whose work you know very well. After the talk's done, you may be pleasantly surprised to find people raiding the store for your backlist and asking for your signature.

- *Speak or guest-teach at a local school or college.* All these places are eager for visiting writers, for an hour, a few days, and sometimes longer. If you like kids, it's a lot of fun—as is the feeling that you can talk to them about books they'd actually be excited to read. I've briefly guest-taught at local public schools for free, but for other places, I charge an honorarium and travel expenses.

- *Attend a weekend writing workshop.* Whether it's a two-hour freebie or a two-day master class, participating in a class can bring friendships with other writers, as well as give you new ways to work better at your craft.

- *Teach a "how to get published" course.* People ask you this all the time, so why not tell them to come to your class? County extension services and local writers' organizations would be hungry for your expertise.

- *Get to know the Friends of the Library committees in your area.* Let them know you're available to participate in fundraising events such as author nights. Connect with librarians who coordinate book clubs and author talks. Suggest yourself and author friends for an event. Many libraries have a small budget for speakers, so you may make a few hundred dollars here and there.

- *Host a regular mystery book club discussion group at a local bookstore or library.* Yes, you will be discussing other authors' work, but you will be growing the store owner's and book club members' commitment to you. Imagine the turnout when you finally have a book signing.

Remember—readers are your ballast, in fair weather and foul. Stay connected to them and they will support you!

COMMITTING TO MY DREAM

EDITH MAXWELL

I recently stepped off the edge into a new adventure, as a friend put it. Others might call it plunging into an abyss or committing to a dream, but we'll get to that.

I've wanted to be a published author of mystery novels for more than two decades. A few years ago, when I was laid off my job as a technical writer, I decided to finally write that book. I'd had several short stories published in reputable anthologies, and my sons were launched into their own lives. I started to write a mystery, continuing after I secured a new job. I finished it, polished it, had it critiqued, and endured dozens of agent rejections and unreliable small presses, including a fraudulent one. I persisted, however, and now I have not only a series with an excellent small press, but also an agent and a series contract with a big publisher.

During these recent years, I also worked full time in high tech in the Boston area. I awoke before five, drove an hour to work and an hour home, exercised, cooked dinner, and then collapsed with a glass of wine and the newspaper. Fiction was relegated to weekends and retreats. I made a three-year plan to leave the day job.

But I was stressed out. I wanted to pursue my authorial dream with more time, energy, focus. I read an article in the

New Yorker that said, "If you can do something risky that you think will improve your life, you ask, what's the worst that can happen?"

I'm of a certain age, but not quite certain enough to draw Social Security or Medicare. Still, I have some savings. My expenses are pretty low because last summer, Hugh and I sold our too-large house and bought a smaller house for cash. I live in Massachusetts, which provides low-cost health care to those who need it.

So in May 2013, I committed to being a mystery author. Only one year into my three-year plan, I resigned my well-paying job in the software industry. So far, I'm loving it. My commute is one minute to my upstairs office. I get more exercise. I crank out words every morning and do other writing-related tasks in the afternoon, like preparing blog posts and writing essays called "Committing to My Dream." I turned in my second Local Foods mystery on time. I sent in *Bluffing Is Murder*, my second Speaking of Mystery manuscript. I'm on schedule writing *Farmed and Dangerous*, the third in the Local Foods series. I'm plotting a third series, an historical I now have time to research. I'm able to give back to my support groups: Sisters in Crime, the Salem Writers Group, the SinC Guppies, and my Wicked Cozy Authors blog partners.

Taking this plunge was nerve-wracking. I don't have as much of a financial cushion as I'd like. Because of twenty-four-hour access to the kitchen, I'm acquiring quite a physical cushion. And the usual fears abound: Maybe my contract won't get renewed. No one will want the new series. My sales will plummet.

But what's the worst that can happen? I get another job,

whether tech writing or bagging at Trader Joe's. I take Social Security earlier than I intended or I move in with a son when I'm ninety. I can deal with all of that.

And what's the best? I get to write mystery fiction all day, every day.

Stepping off the edge into the adventure—or the abyss, as the case may be—might not be for everyone. For me, committing to living my dream was the right choice.

PSSST: COMMIT TO YOURSELF (PASS IT ON)

CHRIS ROERDEN

I love mysteries, but I don't aspire to write them. And despite producing thousands of critiques, hundreds of handouts, and the occasional article, I'm not driven to write nonfiction. Except twice.

After one summer's teaching in South Korea, my head and heart remained so profoundly enraptured by the people and places, I could concentrate on nothing else. I had to write that story. (My eighth book.) *Wish someone had whispered to me: Stop hesitating. Commit to your passion.*

The second time, on realizing my teaching notes would someday be nothing but ashes, like me, I dragged myself from my comfort zone to publicly expose what I knew about editing. I feared the criticism from bigger names than mine. *Wish someone could have whispered in my ear: Face your fear. Accept discomfort. Take risks.* Eventually I did. (Books ten and eleven resulted.) *Risk-taking changes your life. It really does.*

I believe that how we identify ourselves reinforces our identity. I write, but I don't identify as a writer. I'm an editor (full time) and writing instructor (part time)—roles often sharing the same workday (double time?). Like you, I have other identities, too. (My fondest: grandma.) But not every role merits equal time. Or prime time. *Two whispers I must constantly repeat to myself: Prioritize. Focus.*

After my first ten years in publishing, I took time out for motherhood. I also wrote my first book (an editing commitment for an absent manuscript), earned an MA, and started toward a PhD but discovered the women's movement instead. For the next ten years of domesticity, I worked for equal rights—which became its own full-time commitment. All these labors of love utilized skills from my editing career-on-hold: analyzing, organizing, communicating.

When my two offspring reached college age, I returned to publishing. As managing editor, I encountered community leaders who remembered my volunteerism. *Whispered reality: Membership creates contacts; volunteering creates loyalties at all levels.*

Women who'd known me now ran companies, which generated written materials. Which needed editing. The commitment to *me* of those businesswomen helped me become independent. I was in business! An entrepreneur! *For your ears, I whisper: We're all entrepreneurs. If you write, you run a writing business. Its sole client is you. Commit to supporting your single most important client.*

Because I'm committed to helping writers write better, I got into the business of doing precisely that. Being the managing editor of someone else's business derailed my mission. *Whisper: Identify your core mission.*

A mystery writer once told me how much his series depended on his freelance editor. The next year, the freelance editor quit to pursue her own mission: writing *her* mysteries.

Whisper: Honor your mission by committing to it.

Like most businesses, mine requires record keeping, time management, deadline meeting, and (unlike the freelance editor who quit) maintaining the expectation of open-for-business reliability. *Whisper: If you commit to writing, you are a writer. Remain committed. Writing is hard work. Writing what others want to read is harder. Give it time. Lots.*

Initially I'd experimented with subcontracting routine editorial work to freelancers, but in spot-checking the results, I ended up re-editing their work. *Wish someone had whispered to me: Never subcontract part of your core mission.*

Likewise, you don't want to delegate your writing. (Forget James Patterson.) Might you subcontract research? Probably. Revision and critiquing? Certainly. Typing, housecleaning, babysitting, blogging? Absolutely. Whatever is affordable. I now delegate business tasks only: list maintenance, tax preparation, culling resources that keep me current in my field, and so on.

Wish someone had whispered practical information in my ear. I hope I would have known enough to listen.

COMMITTING YOURSELF!

KELLI STANLEY

Commit. Commitment. Committing.

One thing you might have noticed with this project is that we're sticking to gerunds—you know, those wondrous combinations of noun and verb that impart and imply a certain immediacy, a kind of ongoing and present act.

Let's hear it for the gerund! Because *committing* is an ongoing, present (and crucial) act in your writing and in your life.

Notice how "commitment" looms large in the modern lexicon. We often hear about the boyfriend/girlfriend who is "afraid of commitment." (Can you hear me, George Clooney?) Marriage laws have changed in much of the world in order to allow people of the same gender to make a legal commitment to one another—that is, get married. And, of course, when you find your car with a flat tire in the driveway while you're desperately trying to figure out the problem with the last third of the manuscript and must, instead, call a tow truck . . . well, you might just say, "Commit me"—and I don't mean to George Clooney.

So "commitment" connotes something serious. Love, marriage, even a trip to the local mental health facility. It's a somewhat intimidating noun, which is why I prefer the much less scary "committing."

Committing is vital. Vital to starting a manuscript, vital to finishing a manuscript, and vital to keeping alive hopes, dreams, and ambitions once you're published.

I'll be honest. I know and understand the challenges to committing to something—and to committing to yourself most of all. Before I secured my first publishing contract, I was afraid to join Sisters in Crime or Mystery Writers of America or any other organization. Despite enormous support from my beloved family, I was afraid to invest in myself.

I thought, "Maybe I'm just delusional" (thinking of the previously illustrated definition of "commitment," perhaps). I thought, "Maybe I'm not really a writer; maybe I'm not really a good writer; maybe I'm never going to be a successful writer."

Note: These are thoughts that never actually disappear. Most crime fiction writers I know, from *New York Times* best sellers on down, face the same doubts with every book.

So at least I was in good company, though at the time, I didn't know it.

What I felt is what most of us feel when we do something new and different and terrifying and wonderful and, most especially, something we want to do. Because we love to write, we feel guilty. We should be spending our time doing things we don't want to do, right?

Wrong.

At some point, you commit to writing. First a page, then a section, maybe a chapter. And then you commit to finishing. Then, finally, you commit to publishing. Then you commit to writing again, and to trying to stay alive and successfully so in a highly volatile, unpredictable, and nobody-knows-the-magic-formula-to-bestsellerdom industry. The challenges—at the beginning, middle, and even top—are formidable.

So do it. Take the plunge, wherever you are with whatever

project you're working on. Hold your breath, close your eyes, take the leap of faith. You must have faith in yourself, and—if that's hard—remember that others have faith in you and *you* have faith in *them*.

Commitment is scary, I know. But it will change your life. And it will change you.

Because flat tires come and go, but what's inside of you—the work you create and the love you pour into it—will live forever.

Commit to yourself. It's a beautiful thing.

And you're worth it!

CONVINCING

"Without ambition one starts nothing.
Without work one finishes nothing.
The prize will not be sent to you.
You have to win it."
— *Ralph Waldo Emerson*

A MATTER OF CONVICTION

LAURA DISILVERIO

I have a writer friend who worried constantly about whether or not she was a "real" writer. (And, no, this is not one of those hypothetical friends who looks a lot like me.) While she worked on her first novel, she insisted she wasn't a real writer because "real writers are published." After she got her first book published, she worried that she wasn't a real writer because "real writers don't need day jobs"; they support themselves strictly with their prose. You get the picture. Her image of a real writer (apparently some sort of cross between J. K. Rowling and Jonathan Franzen) changed every time she achieved the milestone she had previously identified as epitomizing a real writer. Nothing I could say would convince her that she was an honest-to-goodness writer because she *wrote*, because she worked on her craft.

I never had that problem. I was convinced from the moment I plunked my behind in my desk chair and began to work on a novel, mere days after I retired from the Air Force, that I was a writer. Even though it took me more than two years to land an agent and four and a half years to sign a book contract, I identified myself as a writer. Through the hundred-plus rejections, the pints of Ben & Jerry's, the classes, and the revisions, I thought of myself as a writer and introduced myself as such. Why, then, you ask, am I writing this essay?

Because I wasn't convinced that what I wrote was meaningful or worth reading. I write amateur sleuth and PI mysteries. They're all humorous and relatively light: no sadistic serial killers, graphic sex and violence, or protagonists as likely to pickle themselves in Jim Beam as go out and solve a case. They're not the kind of books that win Pulitzers or even Edgars. Even with twelve books published, I struggled with the idea that I should be using my talents to write "serious" books, novels that explored the meaning of life while confusing readers with unreliable narrators, dense prose, and tortured metaphors; novels that took my protagonist to Hades without a return ticket and ended either ambiguously or tragically; novels that would require me to have a new headshot where I dressed in black and smoldered at the camera, unsmiling, unapproachable, inscrutable.

It took an email from a reader to finally convince me that what I was writing was worthwhile. This fan's sister had gifted her with signed copies of two of my books while she was in the hospital—not in her hometown—recovering from being struck by a car. She wrote to me when she returned to her home, mostly healed, told me my books had helped with her recovery, and ended with a thank you for "a read that leaves you feeling good—a great comfort read."

I teared up. (Okay, I bawled.) It was such a moment of affirmation. I realized it was a gift to be able to make people feel good, to make them laugh. It convinced me that I was using my God-given talent rightly. Not to say I don't need reconvincing occasionally, because I do. But I saved that email, and every time I get to feeling my next book should feature a protagonist that Al Pacino or Glenn Close (think *Fatal Attraction*) could play in the movie version, I read the email, smile, and start trotting out the slapstick, the hyperbole, the slightly damaged but endearing characters, and the happy endings.

THE "IT'S ALL CRAP" STAGE OF THE CREATIVE PROCESS

CATHY PICKENS

Whether a book or an article, I would breeze through that first draft—after much planning, of course. The writing, on lots of days, would flow. When it was done, I would be excited to go back and discover what was written there, certain that *this* time, I'd figured it out, conquered the demons that had plagued me in the past. This time, all that obsessive planning and outlining would pay off, I was sure.

But, no. There it would be. What I began to call the "it's all crap" stage of the creative process.

I would fling myself dramatically onto the sofa, moaning to my husband that my writing life was over, that I'd never again create anything worth reading. Okay, most of the moaning was in my head. But the twinge of fear was very real.

Eventually, I would sit down and get to work, figuring I had to find a way to fix it. I'd nibble around the edges, chip away at the ugly bits, keep working.

One day, immersed once again in the process of rewriting, I realized—it *always* happened. Not just with my writing. Whether as a kid, learning a new piece of music or a dance step, or in my professional life, designing a new consulting presentation, I *always* hit the "it's all crap" stage.

After an intense five-year study of the creative process, I'm convinced that most artists encounter the all-crap stage, no matter their medium. The best ones learn to shove on through. And that's the secret: not dancing around it, ignoring it, or pretending you can plan enough to avoid it completely, but pushing on through.

I wanted it to be easy. I wanted to somehow unlock a secret that made it flow and made it good and made it fast—like an Easy Bake Oven. (An oven powered by a light bulb is a bad example, but you get the idea.)

I eventually realized I needed to trust the process. The work *is* the process. In reality, the crap stage represents the place where we have something to work with, something to mold, something we *can* make good.

I also came to realize that dreaded stage may be what prompts writers' endless fascination with outlining. My husband once asked why, in an audience of writers, someone inevitably raises a hand and asks, "Do you outline?" He can't understand the grail-awe that question holds for writers. Secretly, we think someone else must have figured out a magical way to avoid the thing we all dread.

After I'd been writing for a while, I discovered Anne Lamott's brilliant book *Bird by Bird: Some Instructions on Writing and Life* (Pantheon, 1994), in which she explains the necessity of producing "shitty first drafts." I take that to mean that dreading what I call the crap phase can, for some people, get in the way of producing anything at all. That makes it a serious, systemic problem, I'd say. (Our use of fecal terminology I'll leave to the analysis of others.)

The more I studied the process of other writers and artists, the more I realized no amount of outlining or planning or hoping could make that stage less crappy or easier to fix, that it just *is*. Can't say I've learned to love it, because I keep hoping I'll discover a secret way to avoid it. Until then, head down, focused, chipping away at the bad bits, at least I have something to work with.

BUY THESE BOOKS OR THEY'LL KILL ME!

PATRICIA SPRINKLE

Why am I writing about how to convince people to buy my books? If I were wildly successful at it, would I be writing this? No, I would be on a cruise. Besides, for me, convincing people to buy my books ranks right up there with putting my grandchildren on a sidewalk and begging everybody who passes, "Like these kids. Please like these kids."

Unfortunately, no book gets bought unless somebody is passionate about it, and that somebody is usually the author—even if it costs more to convince people to buy the book than the author earns. For one signing in my hometown before the advent of email, I printed and mailed postcards to everybody I knew. People came in droves. The store made money. The publisher made money. My royalties were two dollars *less* than I had spent on the cards. My husband warned on the way home, "We can't afford too many successful signings."

I informed him, "This is getting my name out there. Those who don't buy today may buy tomorrow." Memorize that. It is the author's mantra.

I'll let other authors extol the virtues of blogging, Facebook, and other social media to sell books. Here are four simple things that work for me.

1. *Speaking engagements.* The number of groups looking for a program each month is staggering. I've accepted invitations from anybody who asked, even for a family reunion of cousins I didn't know I had. I always ask if I can bring books to sell. Tacky? If you're afraid of being tacky when trying to sell your books, you are in the wrong business. I never presume the attendees will go home and order. I offer them a book right then and another with a personal inscription to their favorite aunt. In addition, I learned to ask how many people a group expects after I went to what I thought was a cozy retired teachers' sorority and they had two hundred members. The ten books I had taken along sold very quickly. I have also learned the advantages of ordering books through a local bookseller. I offer them a guaranteed sale at 75 percent of the sales price. They make some money, I make some money, my sales count toward my royalties, their sales count against their returns, and I've made a bookseller friend who will hand sell my books. What's not to like?

2. *A database.* Send me a joke email with all your friends' names on it, and they'll hear from me the next time a book comes out. I am a rabid collector of email addresses. Yes, I pass out a sign-up sheet for names and email addresses at every speaking gig. I wish I had thought to do it in kindergarten.

3. *A team.* After several bookstore signings where I spent an hour giving directions to the restroom and a signing where nobody came except the best man from our

wedding, I discovered the wisdom of teaming up with other authors. Not only does it usually make for a better program, but some of their readers may buy my books.

4. *A simple-to-use website.* My son the website optimizer advises that the fewer clicks they have to make, the more likely they are to buy a book. To my utter astonishment, he is right.

Finally, I wear a big black button that says, BUY THESE BOOKS OR THEY'LL KILL ME! I have no reliable data that it inspires people to buy books, but it gets laughs. I find that people who laugh are more likely to buy books than those who don't.

MY CONVINCING CALL TO ACTION

ROCHELLE STAAB

*"If you go to work on your goals,
your goals will go to work on you."*
—*Jim Rohn, American entrepreneur, author, and
motivational speaker*

A cliché drove me to launch my writing career. Another cliché gets me to the keyboard every day. Hey, I'm as fond of tired phrases and worn gestures as the next guy.

My dream to become an author started with poetry in my angst-y twenties and graduated to an unfinished screenplay in my flamboyant thirties. When I hit my forties, I bought a "how to write a romance" book with the intention of becoming the next Nora Roberts. Not my best idea, based on my bumpy romantic history. Then my first love, mystery, came calling.

With each phase, I announced my ambition to family, friends, and coworkers ad nauseam. What fun is a dream when you don't let the world in on the plan? I envisioned myself at the keyboard hammering out books by the shelf-load. Meanwhile, in real life, I mastered every excuse to avoid writing. The demanding real job. Too much to do at home. Tomorrow. First thing in the morning. While on vacation. When I get back from vacation. After the holidays. After a nap.

I always had a plot churning in my head—that was the easy part, right? I simply had to put the story to paper. Thinking about writing was so much easier than writing.

One stress-filled afternoon at the Real Job, I wandered into the break room to dodge the queue of unanswered emails in my inbox and ran into my buddy Ed. Ed, a fellow dreamer, launched into a reverie of things-he'd-rather-be-doing than return phone calls. And for the three-hundredth time, I brought up the novel I planned to write.

Ed rolled his eyes.

Every swaggering boast, every empty promise, every unwritten manuscript, flushed my cheeks with hot shame. He didn't believe me. I wasn't fooling anyone except myself. Worse, I wouldn't let anyone down but me. That was the moment I became convinced to become a woman of my word and take action. Write—or let go of the fantasy.

The next day, I enrolled in a writing class. I found my tribe in that classroom of writers and never looked back.

Today writing is my Real Job. I'm wise to the shallow excuses I made for so many years to dodge the blank page. What is convincing me to ignore my internal slacker and sit down to write every day? Another old cliché: Just Do It.

Write.

Oh, you say you have a legitimate excuse not to write today? I'm rolling my eyes.

Just do it. For you.

ENJOYING

"All happiness depends on courage and work."
— *Honoré de Balzac*

"Twenty years from now you will be more disappointed
by the things that you didn't do than by the ones you did do.
So throw off the bowlines. Sail away from the safe harbor.
Catch the trade winds in your sails.
Explore. Dream. Discover."
— *H. Jackson Brown Jr.*

IT'S ALL ABOUT THE JOY

JUDY CLEMENS

A few years ago, I hit a writing wall. I was trying to get published in a new genre and reading age group, and was working madly to that end. I had an agent, but nothing sold. Each day, I searched my inbox for more bad news. Rejections, one after another. I told my agent not to even send the editors' responses anymore, because each time I saw the words, "Thank you for sending us Judy's novel, but . . . ," it killed my motivation, my work ethic, and my joy for the day. So much for getting any more writing done. I became so used to the whole negative process that whenever I saw my agent's name in my inbox, I was sure it was another rejection. Only 50 percent of the time was I right. But that's where I was in my head.

I began to see the rejection letters as statements of my worth. Writing had become the only way in which I judged myself. If I wasn't selling what I really wanted to sell, what was the point of it all? Why did I sit down at the computer each day? It wasn't even fun anymore.

That's when I realized the problem. *It wasn't fun anymore.* My writing had become about one thing—getting published. It was no longer about getting to know the characters, or figuring out the plot, or even the physical and mental act of the writing itself. I had one goal, and that colored everything about the whole process. I took a good look at what my work—and I—had become. Nothing looked like what it should. What is the point of writing, or any career, if it no longer brings joy? Something had to change.

I concentrated on my adult mysteries. I amicably parted ways with my agent (we're still friends). And I remembered that I was writing things in other genres and reading age groups because *I loved those books.* Sure, I still wanted those books to be published (still do), but if that was the sole purpose of it all, it wasn't worth being miserable most of the time and dreading my time at the computer. What needed to change wasn't whether the books were getting published or not. What needed to change was my attitude.

I still work with the eventual goal of seeing my books published, but each day when I write, I enjoy spending time with the characters and seeing the story take shape. I write because I love writing and I love books. If the books get published, all the better. But until then, it's got to be about the joy.

Enjoy the day. Enjoy writing. Because that's the biggest part of everything you do.

FUN

BARBARA D'AMATO

When I became involved with Sisters in Crime in 1986, it was mainly because I was annoyed at the lack of reviews of women's mysteries in the media. For one person to complain was not very effective. But the word of a large organization would have real power. What I had not anticipated was that my writing would be enriched. I had not expected the little gems that being involved in SinC made possible.

Like this one:

The late Hugh Holton—mystery writer, SinC member, and Chicago cop—and I were driving back to Chicago after presenting a Sisters in Crime lunch program at a library in southern Illinois. We saw a roadside farmers market and decided to stop. I bought a bag of tomatoes and went to find Hugh, who was at the honey stand looking for a present for his mother. The stall had a large *B*, a painting of a bee, and the names of the stall holders, something like Bill and Betty or Ben and Babs. The stall holders, who were probably husband and wife, were pointing out the virtues of their honey. Buckwheat honey, the wife said, was rich and best for cooking, but for pouring on waffles and pancakes, she'd advise the clover honey.

"Both from our own fields or neighbors'," the husband said.

"Or blueberry honey. It's tangy and fruity," the wife said.

The husband added that they had a friend about ten miles away who grew blueberries.

Hugh looked at another shelf. "Orange blossom honey?"

"Not ours," said the wife.

"Imported. From Florida," said the husband, more disparaging than admiring.

Well, sure. We don't have many orange groves in Illinois.

"No oleander honey," said the wife, who may have had a devilish streak.

Hugh asked why not.

"Oleander honey is poisonous. Oleanders are poisonous, and if the bees make honey from a lot of oleanders, the honey is poisonous."

"No oleanders in Illinois," the husband said. "Oleanders are Californian."

Hugh and I managed not to look at each other, but we were both thinking, *I can use this!*

Hugh bought both buckwheat and clover honey and we started back to my car. Partway there, we began to chuckle.

I couldn't count the gems that have come my way since joining Sisters in Crime. There are innumerable places I wouldn't have seen, people I wouldn't have met, and facts about the world I could never have known enough to research. I've learned that while working hard on your manuscript is a must, to a certain extent you have to relax and let the gems come to you. You have to be open.

Then you realize, *I can use this.*

CELEBRATE GOOD TIMES

KIM FAY

I come from a family that loves to celebrate. Give us a new baby, birthday, or wedding; throw in pies, potluck, and karaoke; and we're happy campers. It was only natural when my novel, *The Map of Lost Memories*, was finally published—fourteen years and umpteen drafts after I started it—that I did what any self-respecting Fay would do: commandeered an art gallery, filled it with wine and hors d'oeuvres, brought in my favorite bookseller, and welcomed seventy-five of my nearest and dearest to help me rejoice in my dream coming true.

I know a lot of writers who are uncomfortable enjoying their successes. But the way I see it, writers don't have unlimited opportunities for unadulterated enjoyment. Most of our time is spent alone, forcing ourselves to sit at the computer, agonizing over sentences and plot. And then there are the publishing blues. Will I or won't I be published, or, now that I am published, will anyone like my book? So when chances come along to throw your arms wide and dance, I say dance away. It feels good, but even more so, you might just find yourself in the company of others dancing with happiness, too.

Case in point: One morning in January, I received an email from the marketing manager at my publisher. "Hi Kim, I just heard the Edgar news and wanted to send my congratulations!

Well done." No one in the history of the Internet has sent a search through Google as fast as I did at that moment. There it was, the news that *The Map of Lost Memories* had been nominated for the Edgar Award for Best First Novel by an American Author. The room twirled. My pulse snapped. I called my mom. I called my agent. Then I started dancing.

But my jubilation mingled with confusion. My book had been categorized as many things—historical, literary, adventure, suspense. Never, though, mystery. The Edgar nomination came out of the blue, and I wondered, was I a fraud? I wasn't really a mystery writer. Or was I?

As the months passed, I decided to ignore my doubts and just keep dancing. I attended mystery panels and Sisters in Crime meetings, and no one accused me of being an emperor with no clothes. In fact, I was welcomed with open arms. And the more at home I felt, the more I was reminded that as a kid, I read mysteries, I wrote mysteries, and I even put in time as an amateur sleuth, digging through the school janitor's pickup truck for evidence—of what, I can't recall. As I got older, my writing veered down a different path, but suddenly, now, at the age of forty-six, that old road was cutting in front of me, and I wanted to follow it.

When May came around, I sat at the Edgar banquet and lost, and I was thrilled. I had been nominated for one of the country's top book awards. But better yet, that nomination had drawn me into a world of people who, as far as I could tell, understand the importance of enjoying the entire experience of being a writer. We meet up at book festivals. We eat gumbo together. We have online groups where we cheer each other on. We are unpublished and we are best sellers, but that doesn't seem to matter. What matters to them—and what they've taught me—is that you shouldn't just sit around waiting for a reason to dance to come along. When you're not at your desk, get up and make a reason, and be sure to surround yourself with people who want to trip the light fantastic with you.

SMELL THE ROSES...OR RACE FUEL

TAMMY KAEHLER

I'm an overachiever. I figure most writers are or we wouldn't have the gumption to make it over the hurdles put in the way of our work being read by an adoring public. As overachievers, we think we can do it all. Have it all. Often, however, we overestimate our abilities or underestimate the size of the task.

I knew writing the book was going to be the hardest part for me, and though I wasn't wrong, I didn't realize how much work the promotion side of "being an author" would be. I'd been a writer, a public speaker, and a marketer my entire career, so I figured I had all the tools: knowledge, experience, enthusiasm. I was ready to promote the hell out of a book.

And boy, did I try.

When my first book was published, I wrote dozens of guest blog posts, traveled thousands of miles for signing events, did radio interviews, spoke to book club meetings, sent out newsletters, and kept up with Facebook, Twitter, Goodreads, Pinterest, and Instagram. I ran myself ragged. When my second book was published, I was still tired. I scaled back, didn't do as much . . . and I realized I enjoyed it a whole lot more.

The words that had played on an endless loop in my head that first year were, "I *could* do xyz, so I *should*." I knew I *could* write witty and engaging newsletters and blog posts. I knew I'd be good on panels. I knew I'd stay visible to the mystery community by keeping up with social media. But gradually, I buried my good humor—and some days, my will to live—under a litany of shoulds. Worse, trying to accomplish every item on my list began to take up all of my time, keeping me from the most vital task of all: writing my next book.

Logically, I knew I couldn't do everyth— Wait a minute, I was trying to do everything. I hadn't even been listening to myself. I took a couple steps back from the to-do list, reevaluated, and developed a brand new mantra: "Just because I can doesn't mean I have to."

I decided to focus on what I actually liked doing and ignore the stuff I didn't—no matter how much that stuff worked for other people, no matter how well I knew I could do something. If I didn't want to do it, it was off the list. Facebook? Yes. Goodreads? Gone. Bookstore signings? Not in every possible city, but only where I have family. Newsletters? Not every month, but only when I've got something to say.

The choices freed me. First, I had more time because I did less and wasn't bogged down by the guilt of not doing more. Second, stepping off the merry-go-round of "this is what everyone else does" gave me time to pursue opportunities unique to me. I traveled to races for signings. I connected with racing fans and bloggers. I even got invited to write for a blog site centered on women in racing.

Third, and most important, I developed a routine of marketing and promotion activities that was manageable while I got back to writing another Kate Reilly Racing Mystery.

The moral of the story? Do what you enjoy and don't bother with what you don't like. Don't think you have to do it all, otherwise you might miss the one-of-a-kind experiences that come your way. Even worse? You might never get to that next book.

ENJOYING THE WRITING LIFE

CARLA NEGGERS

I'm one of those writers who loves to write. It was the joy of writing that prompted me to climb a tree with a pad and pen as a kid and sit up on my favorite branch to spin stories. Sixty-plus books later, I love to write as much as ever. That doesn't mean it's always easy. A writing life can get out of whack for any number of reasons. No writer I know, including me, is immune. So I asked myself, What do I do that allows me to enjoy writing as much now as when I was a kid? Is there any one thing? Any one practice? The answer is yes: I make time for "discovery."

A few years ago, I took off to Ireland for my own personal writing retreat. It was a spur-of-the-moment trip. Next thing I knew, there I was, alone in a tiny cottage on the southwest Irish coast with my pads and pens, figuring out how to light a turf fire on a rainy, chilly autumn night. My Irish sojourn wasn't a getaway to meet a tight deadline, and it wasn't a vacation. It was three weeks I set aside for creative discovery—for consciously and intentionally standing back from producing, doing, inventing, measuring, making things happen. It was time away from the usual walls: page counts, word counts, hours-at-writing counts. It was time away from the external lures and pressures of publishing, platforms, website updates, reviews, Facebook, Twitter, wandering on the Internet.

My cottage made setting these boundaries for myself easier: It had no Wi-Fi and only limited (and expensive!) data roaming access. I had to walk into the village to get on the Internet. The five-hour time difference between Ireland and the East Coast also worked in my favor. There's magic in being fully present in the moment, whether it's on the page at hand or in walking in the Irish hills, listening to sheep baaing in a green field, or watching a rainbow arc over the bay.

Those three weeks in Ireland crystalized for me just how important discovery is in my creative life. I have always given myself time away from producing and doing, whether it's an afternoon walk, an Internet blackout, not counting words and pages—or another getaway to an Irish cottage. Discovery is what sharpens, greases, and fires up our creative gears, our senses, our powers of observation, our openness, even our trust in whatever drove us to write in the first place. For me, it's the foundation of creativity, and it's essential to the joy of writing.

A WAKE-UP CALL
TO REMEMBER WHY WE WRITE

GIGI PANDIAN

When I first started writing a mystery, it was a fun hobby. I enjoyed sitting at a café with a friend and a good cup of coffee, playing around with crafting a puzzle plot with plenty of adventure, like the books I love to read. After signing with an agent, I assumed my writing life would be even better. But that's when the waiting began. My critique partners, writing competition judges, and my agent believed in my book, so why was it was taking so long to sell? The innocent fun of writing started to be overshadowed by apprehension.

Then, while my agent was pitching the book to publishing houses, I was diagnosed with aggressive breast cancer. It was the month after my thirty-sixth birthday. It was the wake-up call I needed to remember *why* I was writing in the first place:

- I love the writing process.

- I love my characters and the worlds I create when I write.

- I love being part of the wonderful community of mystery writers I've met.

Once I looked at what I truly wanted from my writing, it no longer made sense to waste time worrying about the frustrations of publishing. Much like my cancer, New York publishing was beyond my control. I knew I needed to focus on things within my control: enjoying my life, including the important writing piece of my life. So what did I do?

- I made my husband promise to tell me if I ever started to let writing stresses creep back into my life. I'm human; it's happened. But in the past year, he's had to remind me only twice.

- I surrounded myself with my wonderfully supportive writers' group. In addition to our usual writing get-togethers (25 percent chatting and 75 percent writing), they took me wig shopping before I started chemotherapy and bought me an amazing mystery-writer style wig.

- I knew I wanted to share my stories with the world, but I wanted to be sure to do it right. I decided to form my own publishing company to publish my first novel. It turned out to be a much bigger project than I ever imagined, but my doctors attributed my success at dealing with some difficult cancer treatments with the fact that I had a positive project to focus on while going through the treatments.

Because I focused on living and writing in ways that were enjoyable, a funny thing happened: I was able to be *more* productive than I ever imagined. Without stress holding me back, I produced even better writing. At the end of that year, not only was I cancer free but I had two traditional publishing deals.

For a brief moment, I wondered what I'd gotten myself into by signing two three-book contracts. I felt apprehension start to creep back into my life. It was time for another reminder: This is my dream. I'm healthy and I'm living it. Damn right I'm going to have fun with these books.

MOVING FORWARD

"Nancy, every place you go,
it seems as if mysteries just pile up one after another."
— Carolyn Keene, *The Message in the Hollow Oak*

"The greatest thing in this world is not so much where we are,
but in what direction we are moving."
— *Oliver Wendell Holmes Jr.*

OUTSIDE IN

LUISA BUEHLER

How different the feeling of knowing you're moving forward and not muddling through. How defining the moment when you understand the difference, not only in your mind but in your heart.

I wasn't published at the time. In fact, I was such a newbie that when I attended meetings, I stood on the outskirts of the "chosen" (published authors) and couldn't bring myself to break the plane and mingle. I listened as Barb D'Amato and Sara Paretsky shared comments from their editors; watched as Hugh Holton and Michael Allen Dymmoch, heads bent close, discussed who-knew-what, but I was sure it was exciting writers' stuff. Had there been a window, my nose prints would have covered it.

At one such event, Barbara D'Amato approached me, introduced herself, and asked, "What are you writing?" I stammered something about amateur sleuth and then stopped cold. *How could I talk writing with her?* She picked up the thread without missing a beat. "Amateur sleuth can be fun to write, but tricky." She scanned the room, spotted a small group of people, and brought me to their side with the introduction, "This is Luisa. She writes an amateur sleuth who solves cold cases. I thought she should meet you."

In the blink of an eye and a gracious introduction, I was chatting with Deb Brod, Mark Zubro, and Hugh Holton. The conversation was truly four-sided, with bits of information passing along from each of us. Deb and Mark, already published, mentioned their issues. Hugh, not yet published, and I, with no agent and mounting rejection letters, expressed our own frustrations.

It was during that exchange that Hugh Holton mentioned one of the best pieces of advice I've received or could ever give. He said that if I hadn't sold the book yet, write the next one and the one after that if necessary. He encouraged me to keep moving my game forward. He said that if I wasn't published after I'd written the second or third book, go back and look at the first book. The more we write, the better we become, he said. After writing another book, I might see what doesn't work in the first one. Or maybe the second book is where the series should begin. I knew I was writing a series, but I had let the rejections stop me from expressing the stories in my head.

I left the meeting knowing that I had moved beyond peering in the window at who I wanted to be. I now was that person—a writer.

THE HOPEFUL WRITER

LUCY BURDETTE / ROBERTA ISLEIB

Before my first book, *Six Strokes Under*, was published in 2002, I absolutely believed the title would appear on the *New York Times* bestseller list. I could picture opening the book review insert and seeing it there, with a small descriptive blurb right underneath the title: "Aspiring golfer Cassie Burdette attends the LPGA qualifying school and finds not only her career on the line—but also her life."

The series never did make it to the bestseller list, though I had some amazing experiences over the course of five books, including playing with two real-life golf pros, meeting some wonderful fans, and having the books featured in a *Sports Illustrated* article. This last piece of great fortune would have sold many, many, many copies had the publisher not remaindered the books at exactly that moment. As you can imagine, this was a blow. And for a while, I struggled with how I would move forward without Cassie, the character I had grown to love like a family member.

With twelve years and twelve books under my belt, I understand more clearly that publishers operate as a business. They can't afford to make decisions based on an author's hopes and passions; they have to base them on sales. An author has to consider both: what might sell and what will fill her with enough excitement to write—and then keep writing.

After the golf lovers mysteries ended, I began to write an advice column series featuring a psychologist in Connecticut. (Write what you know!) That series ended after three books. So I dabbled with a few stand-alone books, before selling a third series: the Key West food critic books, written as Lucy Burdette. I'm writing the fifth book in the series now and beginning to fret about whether the publisher will buy more and what I would write if that doesn't happen.

I came across an interesting article in the American Psychological Association's Monitor on Psychology (apa.org/monitor) that bears directly on my situation. The subject was hopefulness, as distinguished from optimism (a general feeling that good things will happen) and wishing. "Hope is different because it has to do with facing reality," says Jon G. Allen, PhD, a senior staff psychologist at the Menninger Clinic. "As I see it, hope is motivation to stay in the game."

He goes on to explain the three important components of hope: optimism, social support, and setting goals. I couldn't have described any better what I've learned about staying in the publishing game, about moving forward even after you feel like you've hit a wall. There isn't a whole lot a writer can control, at least in the realm of traditional publishing: You can't decide how many books will be printed or where they will be distributed or how much promotion the publisher will put behind your book. You certainly can't force people to buy them and read them and love them and then create a groundswell of sales by telling all their friends.

But you can control how much effort you put into making each book excellent, and doing what promotion is available to you, and planning for where you hope the book will go, and what's next if it doesn't go there. You can develop small goals that point toward your big vision.

And you can surround yourself with friends and colleagues who want to support you and your vision. (Many of my connections have come from my involvement in Sisters in Crime.)

With these tools—optimism, social support, setting goals—along with ABTC (apply butt to chair), I hope to stay in the writing game a long time.

THIRTEEN YEARS

POLLY IYER

I remember the moment thirteen years ago as if it were yesterday. At the time, I owned a home furnishings store. That morning, the store was empty when I loaded in my email. Good thing, because I screamed when I read the message from the editor reviewing my first book. The email has long since disappeared into that trash bin in the ether, but the words on the screen remain burned in my brain:

"I'm on page 49. The story is terrific. The writing needs work."

My eyes locked on the word "terrific." He liked it. He really liked it. "The writing needs work" hit me a few minutes later.

I mention this seminal moment because at the time, I didn't know the extent of what I didn't know. A couple of weeks later, he sent me the first of three edited hard copies and I found out. To this day, I don't think I've met anyone who could tighten a sentence like he could. *But*, since my editor's resume included over forty-two books as a ghostwriter for biographies of famous people, I had no idea what *he* didn't know.

More about that later.

I'd been an illustrator for twenty-five years. Yes, there's a learning curve to art and design. Discipline, technique, media, and a little thing called talent. But nothing compares to the rules and skill building of writing fiction. The one common denominator in reaching a measure of proficiency in either endeavor is the need for perseverance.

Fast forward four years.

A friend in a nearby city called to tell me about an ad she saw in the paper for a meeting of a writers' group called Sisters in Crime. I write crime fiction, I thought. I'm a "sister." So off I went. After a few meetings, two writers asked me if I wanted to join their critique group. I jumped at the chance. They taught me more of what I didn't know. More of what my nonfiction-writing editor didn't know, specifically about POV or head hopping. My novel was full of the internal thoughts of multiple characters in the same scene. Who knew?

As I gained more confidence, I queried agents, received rejections, and, after a couple of years, found an agent who loved what I wrote. Two years of more querying, more rejections, only now they were from editors. I questioned whether I'd ever see one of my books in print.

Perseverance.

By this time, I had a couple of novels under my belt and finally decided to hop on the Amazon bandwagon and publish them myself. I made some mistakes, learned, and before long had published three books.

I could now respond to the inevitable question from a new acquaintance, "And what do you do, Polly?" and answer, "I'm a writer." When they asked the second question, "What do you have published?" or "Where can I get one of your books?" I could tell them where to look with a strong, confident voice.

Fast forward to the present.

I have nine books published, six in my name, three under a pen name, and soon all will be available on every platform and in libraries. Oh, and that first book the editor liked so much? I finally thought it was good enough to publish, thirteen years after I got that email.

"I'm on page 49. The story is terrific. The writing needs work."

And work on it is exactly what I did.

TRANSLATION, PLEASE

HARLEY JANE KOZAK

When I turned in the manuscript for my second novel, I knew I'd be asked for revisions. But when I got an eight-page, single-spaced letter detailing the many, *many* improvements required for my book to be publishable, well . . . (insert blood-curdling screams).

I instantly emailed Ms. Critical, saying, "Wonderful editorial letter. Thanks!" Then I shut off the computer, took to my bed, wept, ate chocolate, got depressed. Reread the letter. Argued with it. Cursed it. Ate more chocolate.

I did not—could not—start the revisions.

Yes, I am thin-skinned. In fact, I'm a baby. A lifetime as an actor has not toughened me up, but it has taught me a way to deal with criticism. Which is what I called upon that dreadful week.

Here's the problem: Not all directors are actors, and not all editors are writers. They may not speak our language. They may see precisely what's wrong with a piece of work without the ability to (A) communicate it kindly, accurately, or with specificity; or (B) offer solutions that don't create more problems than they fix. This inability doesn't make them bad people. They just *seem* like bad people when they say, "I'm yawning my way through this" or "I don't actually like your heroine."

So I translate. Quickly, before their unfortunate words settle into my psyche.

In a film, a director might say, "The scene's flat. I need you to cry at the end." Since I can't order up tears like they're pancakes from IHOP, I translate that demand into the language of emotion. I look to the script or into the eyes of my fellow actor for something to render me vulnerable. Sometimes I have to invent it. And sometimes, I'm sorry to say, if the clock's ticking and the crew's waiting, I resort to, "Harley, remember when Spot was dying, how he looked at you? Remember how soft his ears were?" (Sob.)

Translating editorial criticism is easier if only because I have more than three minutes to accomplish it. Letter in hand, I painstakingly transform each dreadful comment into something positive and concrete and action-oriented. A to-do list. And since I must read and reread this to-do list, it's important that I make it *really cheerful.*

Thus, "Your book's not funny" becomes "Give heroine seven amusing things to say." And "The red herrings aren't memorable" becomes "Add three red herring scenes with fun settings: garbage dump, clown car, mortuary." And "Heroine is whiny" becomes "Find five melancholy heroine lines and make them plucky." The numbers are arbitrary, but they take the job out of the realm of the general and into the land of the specific, which is always where I want to be. And often, a few fixes go a long way.

What I did for novel number two (and still do) was type out my to-do list in fancy fonts and different colors and mount it on beautiful paper, suitable for framing. I added inspirational quotes ("You can fix anything but a blank page"—Nora Roberts) and photos of favorite authors, Mr. Spock, and even my dead mom, yelling encouragement. I played psychic and put in future quotes from Ms. Critical: "Hey, that thing in chapter eight? Love it!" I hung this to-do masterpiece on the wall and told my family not to expect sanity or vacuuming from me until I'd gotten through it.

I filed that horrifying eight-page editorial letter in a box that I locked in a vault that I buried under the floorboards, never to be read again.

And then I could work.

ON KEEPING A JOURNAL

GAIL LUKASIK

For many years, I kept a journal, a place where I could write unfettered by rules and expectations. My journals were a hodgepodge of observations, overheard dialogue, dreams, and reflections on my feelings and experiences. Whatever the day provided, I was tuned in, ready to record it.

A January 1989 entry reads: "The woman sitting behind me on the train hums and snorts. The world as always a little mad at the edges." All I recall about that humming, snorting woman is her twitchy black hair and my fear that she would talk to me. Journal keeping was my way of processing the world around me.

That I kept a journal for years is not surprising. That I stopped keeping a journal is. As I became engrossed in writing mystery novels, my compulsion to note my daily experiences faded. And for a while, I didn't miss it.

Then one day, what every writer fears happened to me. I hit the worst roadblock—writer's block. I'd start a book, stop, start another book, stop, again and again. Somehow I'd lost whatever spark had kept me going through two books of poetry and four mystery novels. I was miserable. Was this the end of my writing career?

A good friend who'd listened to my ongoing laments said, "Why don't you stop trying to write a book and start journaling again? No expectations. Fifteen minutes a day. Just see where it goes. Take a mini vacation from your writing." So kicking and screaming, I returned to journaling. My early entries sound like a ten-year-old wrote them. "Second week of *this* journaling and I don't want to do it." This carping continued for over a month. But I persisted.

About four months into my daily journaling, something unexpected happened. In the middle of my fifteen minutes, I started writing a scene. I'd been complaining yet again about not being able to write and suddenly this sentence erupted: "The old woman had birdlike ankles, which were in sharp contrast to her stark electric hair, white and frightened looking, as if whatever shocked her would not leave her." Dialogue followed. "You should meet my boyfriend," the old woman said. "The stories he tells." "What kind of stories?" I asked. She gestured me closer. "He killed a man." From there, the scene twisted and turned and left me wondering if the old woman's boyfriend was a killer or whether she was demented. And that's how the fourth book in my mystery series began.

Had my countless journal entries about my elderly mother who was in an assisted living facility suffering from dementia transformed into this scene with the old woman with the killer boyfriend? You bet. I'm convinced that I wouldn't have written that scene without the prior months of journaling. By writing daily in a journal and allowing myself to write about anything, with no expectations, I'd gotten back to the basics of writing. Not a task to be accomplished with rules and strictures, but a creative process to be enjoyed and explored.

My return to journaling helped me move forward, rekindling in me that adventurous spirit so necessary to setting out on a blank page with no direction in mind.

TEN THINGS
I KNOW TO BE TRUE

NANCY MARTIN

Thirty-one years ago, I sat down in the armchair beside the fireplace and opened *Publishers Weekly* to discover my very first big-time review. The reviewer skewered me, and as I read her damning words (she called my book "commercial"!), I felt a sharp, sickening pang in my chest that I will never forget. Once I pulled myself together, I was able to better absorb what that particular review had to tell me, and since then, I've reflected a lot on what the world can communicate to a writer as long as I pay attention. Here's what I have learned:

1. The process of writing must be its own reward. The daily ritual of putting words on paper, of telling a story, of creating an emotional response in another person—that is my pleasure. Reviews, awards, and royalties don't really matter. Yes, I pay the mortgage with what I earn from writing, but I would soon be an empty, frustrated, and angry soul if I pursued only publishing contracts or accolades or income. When asked what a writer should write if he wants to make money, Elmore Leonard said, "Ransom notes." I think he meant I must love my process.

2. It's okay to be a nitpicker. In fact, to paraphrase Nora Roberts: Being a paranoid perfectionist makes me a better writer. Good enough is the enemy of great.

3. I was a pantser for ten years before I realized I was a fool not to learn everything I could possibly absorb about my craft and my profession. As much as we wish it to be true, very few of us are natural storytellers. So I started going to workshops and retreats. I built a library of how-to books and refer to it often. (I continue to learn about plot and character and the necessity of conflict. Tension on every page—that's a mantra.) I have come to the conclusion that I wasted a lot of those first ten years of my career. Sure, I wrote books (some sold well and even won awards) and I was well published, but I would not encourage my current readers to seek out that inferior work. I should have learned more sooner. Joseph Campbell's words weren't meant just for fictional characters but for pantsers, too: "The cave you fear to enter holds the treasure that you seek."

4. In the crazy business of publishing, the only thing I can truly control is the quality of my own work. Yes, I keep up with the industry, but I can't be derailed by shenanigans beyond my control. I must ignore the Chicken Littles.

5. That said, it's important to keep up with what else is being written. First, I try to stay ahead of the game, push the envelope a little. And second, reading about current issues that people care about helps me write books that are more than just story. In other words: I must read, read, read. Then synthesize all of it into my own work.

6. I must know my reader. I think about my reader as an imaginary but very specific person: She is a retired schoolteacher—an educated, well-traveled, emotionally intelligent, and warm woman. She has a busy life, and at the end of her day, she relaxes in the bathtub with a smart, witty, entertaining book. I've even given my reader a name. She is Janet. Other writers may write for someone totally different, but I want to surprise and delight Janet with every page. I want to give Janet the experience she wants.

7. I must read my own reviews. Yes, even the bad ones. Perhaps most of all the bad ones. Because really, what kind of person am I if I only want to hear the good stuff? I can pretty much ignore the idiots or readers who simply picked up the wrong book for their taste, but bring on the ruthless critiques. Editors, send me lots of tracked changes. Reviewers, give me your worst! I will use your "commercial" criticisms to become a better writer and a stronger person.

8. I must work every day with a purpose. Writing does have a way of expanding to fill the time allotted, so making forward progress every day—instead of endlessly noodling with what's already written—is key. If I find myself rewriting old pages, it's usually because I don't know what happens next in the story. Think more. Write a daily quota of pages.

9. "When the horse dies, get off." These immortal words, by writer Kinky Friedman, are on a Post-it note stuck on my office wall. To me, they mean that when my book sales start to slip, it's time to reinvent myself. I must not be afraid to

try something new. I have creative ideas aplenty, so why not use them? I can't ride a dead horse.

10. Self-promotion? Even now, after thirty-one years, I still feel the best way to promote my book is to write another book. Janet awaits.

That first review was an eye-opener. I had been a lone writer scribbling in a vacuum, writing whatever pleased me. Hearing at last from an articulate reader was a shock. But I have learned to embrace what the world says about my writing. The main thing? Readers cannot be forced to read what I write. I must seduce them. Charm them, engage them. Be honest and true. I must entertain.

MOVING FORWARD-EVEN WHEN IT FEELS LIKE YOU CAN'T

JUNE SHAW

I have discovered that when life slows you down, you can always still move forward.

I decided I wanted to be a writer in ninth grade. My English I teacher said he was sending me to a literary rally, and since we worked solely on grammar and literature in class, he wanted me to practice writing a paragraph for the upcoming test. He said to write about a splinter.

I mentally confirmed that he was boring, wrote a grammatically correct paragraph describing a sliver of wood, and carried it to his desk. He said *my work* was boring, and I reminded him that he told me to write it.

"No, like this," he said. And he wrote, "Ouch!"

He said to take it from the splinter's point of view. Somebody just sat on it.

Wow, I thought, returning to my desk. A writer could do that? A writer could create any person or thing and make it say or do anything she wants?

Writers don't need to be old dead men from Europe?

I'm going to do that! I want to be a writer!

I placed first in the literary rally—don't even remember what the paragraph topic was—and kept my desire to write. Life was busy. I stayed active in band, home ec, and almost every club offered; spent time with a boyfriend; and lifeguarded and taught swimming lessons. None of my classes had us do creative writing, but I knew that one day, I'd do it on my own. *I'd be a writer.*

As time passed, I'd occasionally think about creative writing. Then I'd pop another baby out. At one time, I had three in diapers. Diapers weren't disposable.

Having five children in six years kept me from having too many thoughts about writing books. I didn't have time to even read any books, that was for sure. My reading came from the backs of cereal boxes, and I did appreciate finding time to absorb those written words while the kids ate.

They were five to eleven years old when their father died.

"I want to be a writer," I said when my brother asked what kind of job I might like. It was a few weeks after my husband had died. I was thirty. I'd married right after finishing high school.

We had little money. I'd need to work, and again that desire erupted: *I want to be a writer!*

But my silly kids wanted to eat and wear shoes, and the main reading I'd done in years listed the ingredients of their chosen cereals. Writing would have to wait.

I needed only a few more hours from our local university, so I completed the work on a BA in English and started teaching English to students in junior high. I enjoyed it most of the time, and I was home when my children were.

The desire kept emerging. That splinter urged me on. I still didn't have time to read, much less write, novels, since I kept up with all my children's activities and had tons of papers to grade.

Eventually I managed short stories and essays. I sold a few! How exciting for me and my family.

By the time I sold a novel, my children were giving me grandchildren and I'd become a caretaker to my mother because of her poor vision.

I now have nine books out!

Recently I sat at my desk and reached for a sheet of paper I'd left on the floor to the right of my chair so I wouldn't forget it. Excruciating pain shot from my back down my left leg to my toes. Weeks of misery led to the determination that I required back surgery.

Pain and having to lie down for two weeks and then not bend or lift crimped my creative juices. I wanted to be writing my next book but couldn't come up with plots or create characters.

Instead, I've done lots of online promotion for my humorous mystery series, which was recently offered as e-books. In addition, Harlequin bought the reprint rights and just published my third mystery in paperback.

The next book I'll create is waiting right in the rear of my mind, soon to surface—for I have discovered that when life slows you down, you can always still move forward.

GIVING BACK

"No matter what accomplishments you make,
somebody helped you."
— *Althea Gibson*

PAYING IT FORWARD

KATE FLORA

I'm not a joiner; my solitary nature is perfectly suited to the writer's life. But a chance meeting with Elizabeth Daniels Squire in 1993, at my first Bouchercon, in Omaha, Nebraska, sent me back home looking for my local chapter of Sisters in Crime. Finding and joining SinC has been one of the most important decisions of my writing career.

Why? At the recent Sisters in Crime Summit in Chicago, we coined a motto for the organization: "You write alone, but you aren't alone." Those few words sum it up for me. For over twenty years, my sisters have been the ones to whom I've turned for advice, support, education, finding an expert, and, most of all, perspective. If you're in this for the long haul, you particularly need perspective—those critical reminders that lots of authors get their series dropped and the world doesn't end, commiseration when it happens, and pep talks about how sometimes you're up, sometimes you're down, and that doesn't mean it's over.

Sisters are there to remind us that being told we need to rewrite isn't the end of the world. That an agent's or editor's rejection is sometimes just one person's opinion, so we need to keep an open mind about the criticism we're getting and not toss the manuscript into the fire. Sisters have read my drafts and given me feedback. They've given me quotes for my books. Now I take real pleasure in reading my new sisters' works and giving them quotes.

Helping sisters build successful careers and being active in the organization and generous with one's time models the best kind of author behavior. Long ago, our chapter started a Speaker's Bureau, and one aspect of that was to pair experienced authors with newbies on author panels. I had the chance to learn from more experienced authors I admired how to play well with others—sharing the mic, making it a discussion, addressing the topic—while engaging an audience and promoting my book. I also learned how to moderate a panel, and how important it is to be familiar with the other panelists' books. These are not small things, as we all know. Learning from our "big sisters" shows us how we should always treat our colleagues, booksellers, librarians, and fans with grace and respect, rather than leave them behind like the car we passed that's now vanishing in our rearview mirror.

It's invaluable, when the majority of your work is done alone, inside your head, to have some help with understanding the business side of writing. SinC does that for us with articles on the changing world of publishing. Locally, chapters help with programs on using social media and marketing. I can turn to my chapter's discussion list to ask questions such as, how do I go about organizing a blog tour? I can ask for help finding an expert. At one point, for example, I needed expertise to write a scuba diving scene. A diving sister read and vetted the scene for me. People at book talks frequently ask how we find cops, lawyers, doctors, and others to help with questions. My answer is, join Sisters in Crime. If a sister can't help you, she can usually direct you to someone who can.

Since an author's career is a steady trajectory of learning and relearning, one of the great benefits of being a Sister in Crime has been the speakers we host and the online classes we make available to our members. We focus on two essential aspects of the job: writing craft and the world of crime. Presentation is also important, and it's not something we can learn at our desks. Very early on, at a Malice Domestic conference, the late Barbara Burnett Smith gave a talk drawn from her business experience on body language and how to engage an audience. Get out from behind that podium, she said, and be accessible. I never stand before an audience without recalling Barbara's advice, and it's been twenty years.

I've been the beneficiary; now I try to also be the big sister who shares. Often, now, I'm on the teaching side of the table—moderating the panels of new authors or giving the class on mystery basics or on creating and sustaining a series character. I'm the one being asked for quotes. I've had the honor of serving on the national board. Locally, I've had the pleasure of watching many aspiring writers become published writers. Each time, I'm reminded of the joys of sisterhood and of one of the founding principles of our organization: that one thing women do well is to network, share, and work together for the benefit of all.

THE BETTER THINGS IN LIFE

BARB GOFFMAN

When I was in college and grad school, I planned to be a newspaper editor. Copy editing appealed to my meticulous side. But my mom discouraged me. Editing didn't pay. I was made for "better things." Yadda yadda.

Ultimately I became an attorney. Mom was happy, but me, not as much. My creative side yearned for freedom. So I began writing on the side and eventually learned about Sisters in Crime. Through SinC, I've met so many others who share my dreams—people who understand that writing, and its sidekick, editing, *is* a "better thing." I began getting my short stories published, and a few years later, I realized my early dream of editing. For the past several years, I've edited the Chesapeake Crimes series with Donna Andrews and Marcia Talley.

But I admit—editing was nerve-wracking at first. An editor is effectively a supervisor, giving feedback, expecting results. Would I be working with authors who cherished every word they'd written and be hostile to the editing process? Would I be dashing the dreams of authors who hoped their words were perfect?

I know firsthand how hard receiving an edit can be.

When I was working on the first draft of my (still unpublished) novel, I received a written critique from the now late Barbara Parker. She'd agreed to read my first twenty pages, and I had been over the moon because she was one of the authors who inspired me to write in the first place. And then I got her edit. Let's just say that my words weren't as cherished by her as they were by me. She highlighted in yellow everything she thought should be deleted—every funny line. She thought my main character should change her job—a job that's integral to the plot. She . . . had issues with my pages. As a result, I slumped. Didn't write for over a month. But then I took a deep breath, reviewed her comments again, took the ones that worked for me, and moved on to write more and better. That's what good editors ultimately should inspire you to do. Write more and better.

It's what I've tried to do for the authors with whom I've worked. Two of them stick in my mind. They each were newcomers. I was the primary editor for their stories ultimately published in *Chesapeake Crimes: This Job Is Murder*. I went through about a half dozen (probably more) rounds of revisions with each of them. Every time I sent another markup, I feared they'd reach their patience limit. I was wrong. Instead, I received responses such as these:

- "I am willing to do whatever it takes to get this baby into shape—just let me know what you think needs to be done."

- "I feel like this moves so much better."

- "I like your tightening and tinkering."

- "I do want to tell you how much I appreciate working with you this way! It is such a pleasure to experience the story coming into a clearer, stronger shape."

- "Thank you so much for your skill, wisdom, experience...and patience."

The last comment stuck with me. These authors thought *I* had patience, when I'd been afraid they'd become sick of me and my continual additional ideas of how their stories could be made better. Their appreciation of my efforts gave me the confidence to not hold back in my editing out of fear of offending an author. As a result, I'm now able to help even more.

Talk about "better things." Editing allows me to make a book or story better, focusing on word choice, tense, clarity, and story development. But I've found something quite unexpected about editing: the joy I get in working one-on-one with other authors, helping them improve their work, letting their talent shine, and ultimately helping their work *be* a "better thing."

BEST ADVICE EVER: DON'T FORGET TO BE HAPPY

J. A. HENNRIKUS

Though the act of writing itself is solitary, being a writer requires community. Community that provides accountability, support, first readers, editors, copy editors, final draft readers, the people who sit in the first row during a reading, and the friends who help promote your book. It takes years to build your writing community, as well as a well-honed skill set to enable you to parse through all the advice.

And there is a lot of advice.

As writers, we need to be open to learning new things all the time. It keeps us fresh, builds our skills, and helps us get out of our own way. I could spend time giving guidance about building characters, the virtues of plotting, techniques for editing, and the importance of research. But there are classes, workshops, online forums, and Sisters in Crime meetings to help with those skills. Instead, I want to share the three best pieces of advice I have received.

First, show up. Be part of the community, not an outsider looking in. And by community, I mean the writing *and* reading community. Be a fan, and pay it forward. Go to readings, take classes, join groups, participate in forums, comment on blogs, like on Facebook, repin on Pinterest, and retweet on Twitter. As a dedicated introvert, I find this the hardest advice to follow. But forcing myself to do just that has made all the difference.

Second, think with abundance rather than scarcity. This can be hard. When friends all have good news and you have none, it takes a strong woman to keep smiling, say "congratulations," and mean it. But once I realized that other writers' good fortune doesn't limit the chances of my own, it reframed everything. In fact, being around success rubs off. And it also helps you remember that success is opportunity meeting preparation. It doesn't just happen.

And third, don't forget to be happy. This advice came to me recently from our own Hank Phillippi Ryan. I was updating her on some good news about opportunities and telling her how afraid I was that I wasn't going to be able to balance it all. She reassured me that I would figure it out, and then she said: "Just don't forget to be happy, today, right now. You've worked hard, and this is great news. Be happy."

In my writing career, my goalposts keep moving. Start a story, finish a story, edit, edit, edit, really finish it, query, submit, edit again, query, submit. And in the meantime, start the next project. But I rarely, if ever, took a moment and allowed myself to celebrate that I'd reached a goal. A goal that at one point felt impossible. I don't mean sending out the news via social media and getting cyber praise from others. I mean really, truly allowing yourself to feel happy, without a caveat.

Don't forget to be happy. I think this is the best advice I could give any writer. All of this—the ideas, the work, the craft—comes from within. And the goals keep moving down the field. So stop and celebrate when it works. It makes all the difference.

MY GUPPY CONNECTION

NORMA HUSS

When I first joined Sisters in Crime, I also joined the Guppy Chapter—before it was an official chapter. Wow! What a revelation. Here were a bunch of sisters (with an occasional mister) who understood me. When I asked my first timid questions, I got understanding and variety, for at the time, there were few already-published Guppies. As my knowledge and confidence grew, I joined subgroups within the Guppies.

In the AgentQuest subgroup, others described happy or sad experiences. I had sometimes contributed answers before, but with this group, I really began giving back. Did anyone have experience with this agent? Yes, I did. I could reply with the wording of my rejection. How about this one? I could point to a website listing requirements. And when the Cozy Gups subgroup searched for published books to study, I often chimed in after reading the first book in a new series. I was giving back and helping other Guppies.

I joined the Goals for Guppies subgroup to do something about my on-again, off-again work ethic. Within this group, I found help that organized my writing life, and also Guppies who needed my help as well. For several months, I took my turn, along with another member, to be an encourager-in-chief. Each week, every Guppy in the group listed her goals, and at the end of the week, she told us how well she'd accomplished them. Then either my co-encourager, Liz, or I, or both of us, would congratulate each of them, chide them, encourage them, or, when goals were missed by a wide mark, possibly suggest they lower their expectations for the following week.

The goals ran the gamut from an hour of writing a week to hours a day on specific manuscripts, blogs, or promotional pieces, plus exercise or meditation or a variety of other individual plans. There were no grades, just gentle comments and cheers for individual achievements. I learned from our most impressive goal setter, Kaye George, who submitted a long page full of goals every week, then usually met them all. She went on to become Guppy president and, no surprise to me, is about to get her fourth series published by a major house. (The invaluable lesson: You put in the time, you get results!)

But gentle hand-patting can only do so much. I remember a week in particular when one Guppy had accomplished almost nothing. She sounded so down. She was discouraged, she wasn't making meals a priority, things weren't going well. Both Liz and I had encouraging words to say. However, I also told her, "This is your mother here. You will eat right. Taking care of yourself is your first goal. It's your only goal this week."

Then I panicked. Who was I to issue such orders? But even before the final verdict came in the following week with her usually cheerful report, including a recount of regular meals, I knew I hadn't overstepped my bounds. I'd answered what was in my heart and what I'd want to hear in the same situation. I'd graduated. No longer was I just someone who merely listened to or replied to other people's information or advice. I was now shouldering responsibility, giving of myself and feeling the satisfaction of knowing I'd been helpful.

The Guppies, originally the Great UnPublished, now include many who became published and stayed around to help their sisters reach the same goal. And now, with mysteries in print, I'm a Guppy who is still learning but also offering any help I can to my favorite group. My most recent "giving back" included the suggestion for anyone in a writing, publishing, or promotion pickle of any kind to "Ask the other Guppies. Together, Guppies know all there is to know—and are willing to share."

IT COSTS YOU NOTHING

DEBORAH J LEDFORD

As a loyal member of Sisters in Crime, giving back to my fellow sisters and misters has always been a pleasure. During my time as president of the SinC Desert Sleuths (DS) Chapter, my door was always open to members with the desire to become published authors. I was able to help make this desire a reality for a number of members as lead editor of the chapter's SoWest series of anthologies.

Each of these titles, featuring original stories written by DS members, provided the opportunity for writers to work at a professional level with editors, meet deadlines, and have their work published and distributed in trade paperback format.

Being showcased in these anthologies became the first publishing credit for a number of writers whose stories were selected for publication. To keep everything fair, the stories were submitted blind, so the editors didn't know the writers until the stories were accepted. I cheered each time a first-timer's name was announced and received exuberant replies from these grateful newbies when they received their "Congratulations, your story has been selected" letters.

The downside to this tale is that, unfortunately, not every story could be accepted, and it broke my heart to send the rejection letters. This was my task as lead editor and a responsibility I didn't relish. The road to publication is often a long one, and my fear of crushing dreams was a heavy burden.

I know all too well the gut-wrenching sadness when a rejection would come my way after crafting what I thought to be the perfect story. Writers need to be patient and soldier on when it comes to believing in their words—often a daunting task. These days, rejections don't get me down. I merely resubmit to a different publication, which often leads to a publication deal. I am now a three-time nominee for the Pushcart Prize, and many of my stories appear in print, many of them award winners.

The Sisters in Crime anthology members who received the rejections were a true inspiration to me. They accepted the bad news stoically and promised they wouldn't give up. I know the importance of these words, and they serve as a reminder each time I sit down at the computer, scared that the words won't come.

Writing can be a lonely profession, and only fellow writers know what it takes to commit, pour out your heart, offer your soul to strangers, and hope the reader will accept what you have to offer. This is another reason to surround yourself with like-minded, supportive, and creative people.

THE LARCOM PRESS
AND LEVEL BEST BOOKS

SUSAN OLEKSIW

There are few opportunities for writers to publish short fiction, and this was something I had hoped to change through a small press I established with a friend. From 1998 to 2003, Ann Perrott and I published the *Larcom Review* and a number of first mystery novels. The *Larcom Review* gave me an opportunity to put into practice certain principles and ideas about life as a writer.

First, every contributor to the *Review* had to be paid and every author of a novel had to receive an advance. They were professionals and needed to be treated as such. We couldn't pay much ($25 for each story, poem, review, essay, interview, photograph, print, or line drawing), especially considering we were the only backers, but we would pay something. Payment was on publication, and no written work was kept on file (to languish, forgotten for years) after the publication of the issue for which it was submitted. Second, every contract had to tilt in favor of the artist. We purchased first North American serial rights and everything else stayed with the artist. After one year, all rights reverted to the writer. Third, we printed the minimum number of copies (1,200) required for the journal to be considered legitimate (whatever that means) by those who assess such things.

By our sticking to these standards, short story writers were able to accumulate enough paid publication credits through the *Larcom Review*, as well as other venues, to qualify for active membership in Mystery Writers of America. No one was paid in copies, though every contributor received a complimentary copy, as well as the opportunity to buy additional copies at a reduced price.

We published seven issues of the *Larcom Review* and five first mystery novels before we ran out of money. This might be a sign of failure, but out of this experience came the very successful Level Best Books and its annual anthologies of crime fiction by New England writers.

In 2003, Barbara Shapiro asked me, "How did you know how to do what you did?" I remember that sentence because I love it but also because it startled me. When Ann and I started out, I didn't know how to do what I did. I had been a freelance editor and ghostwriter, and I had handled page proofs. But the rest of it—selecting and working with writers, choosing and working with a printer, computer book design and layout, selecting paper, distribution and sales, marketing and advertising, contracts, taxes, calculating royalties—was all new to Ann and me.

Ann and I had no idea how to begin, so we just began. We talked to editors of other journals, interviewed designers and printers, talked to paper suppliers, met with freelance editors, and went to bookstores. We learned by asking a lot of questions, and then we learned more by doing. Ann learned, to her surprise, that she was comfortable asking strangers to buy our books and wasn't the least bit upset if a bookstore buyer said no. I learned that I was a terrible poetry editor but loved working on layout and design.

My philosophy was, and still is, that if there's something you want to do, just throw yourself at it. Whatever happens, you'll know more than when you started, you'll be closer to your goal, and your discoveries will open unexpected doors.

GIVING BACK, MOVING FORWARD

PATRICIA SMILEY

My mother gifted me with a legacy of important principles, but two that changed my life were the love of books and the importance of volunteerism. I have donated my time to one organization or another all of my adult life. There is something satisfying about working for free. It unleashes a level of creativity that is sometimes elusive in a nine-to-five job. Over the years, my view of volunteer work gelled into a coda of sorts: (1) love what you're doing, (2) use the experience as an opportunity to learn new skills, especially if they are outside your comfort zone, (3) expect nothing in return except the personal satisfaction of a job well done, and (4) move on when it stops being fun.

When I first toyed with the idea of writing a novel, I took a UCLA Extension class called How to Write a Credible Sex Scene. There, I met a woman who told me about Sisters in Crime. I'd been an avid mystery fan since age ten after reading *Trixie Belden and the Red Trailer Mystery*. Reading, like writing, is a solitary pursuit, and I was eager to learn more about an organization of like-minded book lovers. Soon after joining the Los Angeles Chapter, I volunteered to edit and publish its monthly newsletter. I helped write the chapter's bylaws and became a member of the committee charged with organizing its first writers' conference. Over the years, I continued to volunteer in the crime fiction community, mastering new technology and forging friendships that have lasted decades.

My volunteer work has been met with genuine appreciation, but one of the most meaningful rewards I have received came after I co-chaired a two-day writers' conference in my role as president of the Los Angeles Chapter. Planning the program took two years. The event was a lot of work but also a lot of fun. I found new friendships and strengthened old ones. Two of the biggest names in crime fiction gave the keynote addresses, and I was fortunate to spend time with both of them.

A few days after the conference ended, I received an email from a friend. She had corresponded with one of the keynote speakers, an author whose books had inspired me to write and whom I had naively asked to blurb my first novel ten years before. To my surprise, my friend told me the author remembered demurring on the blurb all those years ago. The author then asked my friend to pass along this message: "Have her ask me again." I could almost hear my mother's voice saying, "Sometimes when you give back, you move forward in ways you never anticipated."

BELONGING

"For surely as each November has its April,
mysteries only are significant;
and one mystery-of-mysteries creates them all:

nothing false and possible is love
(who's imagined, therefore limitless)
love's to giving as to keeping's give;
as yes is to if, love is to yes"

— *E. E. Cummings*

WRITING A NEW FAMILY

LAURIE R. KING

I wrote a book and found a family.

In 1994, *The Beekeeper's Apprentice* told a coming-of-age story of Mary Russell, who meets a retired Sherlock Holmes and becomes first his apprentice, then his partner. Before the fourth Russell appeared in 1998, the first online fan-fiction community had come into being. The Hive, a website, gave way to Letters of Mary, a Yahoo Groups discussion list; a virtual book club started in 2007 (it's still going strong, over on Goodreads). Artwork, videos, Russell costumes, crossword puzzles, needlework, beaded honeybees, and, yes, Russell-and-Holmes tattoos flourish.

And me? I'm just the author. Russell's community welcomes me, of course. They greet me with wide grins (and occasionally schoolgirl squeaks) at cons and events, they friend me on Facebook and listen to my rambles on my blog Mutterings, they come together for virtual parties on Twitter (yes, parties, held at the Russell/Holmes house). Every so often, one of them sits down and writes me an actual letter. Sometimes it feels as if the snowball would roll along just fine without my occasional contribution.

The tech at the root of this vibrant community is a tool: its ease brings us together; its anonymity pushes us apart. Ever been infuriated by the bent head and busy thumbs of a Twitteraddicted dinner partner? Ever known someone reduced to tears by thoughtless online cruelty? Ever realize how long it's been since you actually laid eyes on not just a "friend"—but a friend?

This idea of virtual relationships has been on my mind recently, because one of those friends just died. I spent only a handful of hours in her physical presence during the years I knew her, yet she touched the lives of everyone in the Russell-based community. When she left us, we mourned.

We tend to forget, caught up as we are in the hurly-burly of daily life, the extraordinary nature of our times. To a very real degree, we have taken a step not so much *outside* our physical identities but *in addition* to "real life." We grow families linked not by genetic material but by the connections themselves.

It has been both a great pleasure and a humbling experience to see relationships come into being around something I have done. To know that were it not for my novels, many of these people would never have met, virtually or in real life. Because I sat down one day to tell myself the story of a girl who meets a detective, I am now wrapped up in a community of enthusiastic readers, people who value wit and adventure, people with backgrounds far more interesting than my own. A family, of brothers and sisters in spirit. A family to which I belong.

And as with any family, I belong not just *with* these people but *to* them. They own me. I have responsibilities toward them; the choices I make affect them. After twenty years, I am never unaware of people looking over my shoulder as I write.

However, it is impossible to both write for an audience and remain true to the writing. Any established writer who kills off a beloved character (I haven't—yet) must be prepared for the reaction. That means every time I sit down to put words on the page, I begin by pushing my virtual family's expectations out of the room. Conversely, it means that every time I write, I have to trust that my family will forgive my choices—even those they don't agree with.

Because we are family, and we belong to each other.

ABOUT THE CONTRIBUTORS

SUSAN M. BOYER

susanmboyerbooks.com

Susan is the author of the Liz Talbot mystery series. Her debut novel, *Lowcountry Boil*, is a *USA Today* best seller, an Agatha Award winner for Best First Novel, a Macavity nominee, a 2012 Daphne du Maurier Award recipient, and a 2012 Golden Heart finalist. *Lowcountry Bombshell* was released in 2013, and *Lowcountry Boneyard* is due out in 2015. Susan lives with her husband and an inordinate number of houseplants in Greenville, South Carolina.

LESLIE BUDEWITZ

Leslie is the author of the nationally bestselling Food Lovers' Village Mysteries from Berkley Prime Crime, set in Jewel Bay, Montana, beginning with *Death al Dente* (2013) and *Crime Rib* (2014). "It takes a village to catch a killer." The fun continues with the Seattle Spice Shop Mysteries, coming in 2015. Also a lawyer, Leslie's *Books, Crooks & Counselors: How to Write Accurately About Criminal Law and Courtroom Procedure* (Quill Driver Books) won the 2011 Agatha Award for Best Nonfiction and was nominated for the Anthony and Macavity Awards. She lives in northwest Montana with her husband and their Burmese cat.

LUISA BUEHLER
luisabuehler.com

Luisa writes the Grace Marsden Mystery Series. Reviewers call her style "a cold case sizzle." The stories follow the cold trail of bygone crimes, blending traditional whodunit with hints of romance and the supernatural. The series won the Reader's Choice Award for Best Traditional/Amateur Sleuth, given at the Love Is Murder Mystery Conference. The seventh in the series, *The Reenactor: A Staged Death*, debuted at the *Chicago Tribune*'s Printers Row Lit Fest. Her new endeavor, an adventure story for middle grade boys, *On My Honor*, is out in 2015. Luisa lives in Lisle, Illinois, with husband, Gerry, son, Christopher, and the family cat, Martin Marmalade.

JOANNA CARL / EVE K. SANDSTROM
JoAnna and Eve occupy the same body. JoAnna writes books about chocolate, which Eve just happens to like a lot. Eve is a fifth-generation Oklahoman and a member of the Choctaw Nation of Oklahoma. She is also a former board member and president of Sisters in Crime, and twice served SinC as newsletter editor. JoAnna/Eve graduated from the University of Oklahoma School of Journalism and worked as a reporter, editor, and columnist for more than twenty-five years before retiring to write mysteries full time.

JOELLE CHARBONNEAU
joellecharbonneau.com

Joelle has performed in opera and musical theater productions across Chicagoland. She now teaches private voice lessons and is the author of two mystery series: the Rebecca Robbins mysteries (Minotaur Books) and the Glee Club mysteries (Berkley). Joelle is the author of the *New York Times* bestselling trilogy that debuted with *The Testing* in 2013. Book two, *Independent Study*, followed in 2014, and book three, *Graduation Day*, will hit shelves shortly. Learn more at facebook.com/AuthorJoelleCharbonneau, or twitter.com/jcharbonneau.

JUDY CLEMENS

judyclemens.com

Judy the author of the Stella Crown series and the Grim Reaper mysteries (both from Poisoned Pen Press) and a stand-alone novel entitled *Lost Sons*. She is a past president of SinC and had a great time during her years on the board. To her, one of the best things about writing is the camaraderie and friendships discovered within the community. Have fun!

MEREDITH COLE

culturecurrent.com/cole

Meredith started her career as a screenwriter and filmmaker. She was the winner of the St. Martin's Press/Malice Domestic Best First Traditional Mystery Novel Competition. Her first book, *Posed for Murder*, was nominated for an Agatha Award for Best First Novel. Her second book, *Dead in the Water*, continued the adventures of photographer Lydia McKenzie in Brooklyn. Meredith's short stories and essays have appeared in anthologies and *Ellery Queen Mystery Magazine*. She teaches writing at the University of Virginia.

SHEILA CONNOLLY

Sheila is the Anthony and Agatha Award–nominated author of three *New York Times* bestselling cozy mystery series. Her Museum Mysteries are set in Philadelphia; her Orchard Mysteries take place in small-town Massachusetts; and her recently released *Scandal in Skibbereen* is the second in her Ireland-based County Cork Mysteries. Her romantic suspense e-book, *Once She Knew*, was a *New York Times* e-book best seller and a Barnes & Noble Top 100 Book in 2012. Sheila loves restoring old houses, visiting cemeteries, and traveling when she's not writing.

DEBORAH COONTS

deborahcoonts.com

Deborah's mother tells her she was born a very long time ago, but Deborah isn't so sure—her mother can't be trusted. These things she does know: She was raised in Texas on barbeque, Mexican food, and beer. She currently resides in Las Vegas, where her friends assure her she cannot get into too much trouble. Silly people. She is the author of *Wanna Get Lucky?* (a *New York Times* Notable Crime Novel for 2010 and double RITA finalist), *Lucky Stiff, So Damn Lucky, Lucky Bastard*, and four digital novellas also featuring Lucky O'Toole. Look for her at the bar, but also on her web.

BARBARA D'AMATO

Barbara is a past president of Sisters in Crime and Mystery Writers of America. She won the first Mary Higgins Clark Award, as well as the Carl Sandburg Literary Award for Fiction, the Macavity, the Agatha (twice), the Anthony (twice), and the Lovie (several times). She lives in Chicago.

MADDI DAVIDSON

Maddi is the pen name for two sisters, Diane and Mary Ann Davidson, residing on opposite ends of the United States. The sisters draw on their years in the world of the Big Corporation, experiences imposing complex technology on ungrateful end users, and mutual love of surfing and skiing to pen humorous short stories and novels. They've completed two books in the Miss Information Technology Mystery Series (*Outsourcing Murder* and *Denial of Service*) and are working on the third (*With Murder, You Get Sushi*).

KRISTA DAVIS

kristadavis.com

Krista is the *New York Times* bestselling author of the Domestic Diva Mysteries and the Paws & Claws Mysteries. Several of her books have been nominated for Agatha Awards. Krista lives in the Blue Ridge Mountains of Virginia with a brood of cats and dogs. Her friends and family complain about being guinea pigs for her recipes, but she notices they keep coming back for more. Stop by Krista's website or visit her at facebook.com/kristadavisauthor, twitter.com/kristadavis, pinterest.com/kristadavisbook, mysteryloverskitchen.com, and killercharacters.com.

LAURA DISILVERIO

lauradisilverio.com

The author of twelve mystery novels and counting, Laura is a former Air Force intelligence officer. She writes three mystery series, including the Mall Cop series (Berkley Prime Crime) and the upcoming Readaholics Book Club mysteries (NAL); teaches for Mystery Writers of America University; and served as 2014 president of Sisters in Crime. She plots murders and parents teens in Colorado, trying to keep the two tasks separate.

HALLIE EPHRON

hallieephron.com

Hallie is a New England author of nine mystery-suspense novels and three-time finalist for the Mary Higgins Clark Award. Her work has been called "unputdownable" (Laura Lippman), "unsettling" (*Seattle Times*), "Hitchcockian" (*USA Today*), and "deliciously creepy" (*Publishers Weekly*). Her award-winning *Never Tell a Lie* was made into a Lifetime movie. The *Washington Post* calls *There Was an Old Woman* "a New York suspense story set in an extraordinary outer-borough neighborhood that will stay with readers" and "the perfect thriller lite."

KIM FAY

Born and raised in Washington State, Kim lived in Vietnam for four years and has been traveling regularly to Southeast Asia for more than twenty. A former independent bookseller, she is the author of the historical novel *The Map of Lost Memories*, an Edgar Award finalist for Best First Novel by an American Author, and the food memoir *Communion: A Culinary Journey Through Vietnam*, winner of the Gourmand World Cookbook Award for Best Asian Cuisine Book in the United States. She is also the creator and editor of the To Asia with Love guidebook series. She lives in Los Angeles.

KATE FLORA

kateflora.com

Kate's books include seven Thea Kozak mysteries; a stand-alone suspense novel; the Edgar-nominated true crime story *Finding Amy*, written with Portland Deputy Chief Joe Loughlin; and three Joe Burgess police procedurals. Her fifteenth published short story, "Family Jewels," appears in the anthology *Stone Cold*. Her second true crime, *Death Dealer*, debuts in September 2014, and her police procedural *And Grant You Peace*, in October. Winner of the 2013 Maine Literary Award for Crime Fiction, Kate is a founder of New England Crime Bake, and a founding though former editor and publisher at Level Best Books. She teaches writing at Grub Street.

KAYE GEORGE

Kaye is a short story writer and novelist who has been nominated for Agatha Awards twice. She is the author of four mystery series: the Imogene Duckworthy humorous Texas series, the Cressa Carraway musical mystery series, the Fat Cat cozy series, and the People of the Wind Neanderthal series. Her short stories can be found in her collection, *A Patchwork of Stories*, as well as in several anthologies and various online and print magazines. She reviews for *Suspense Magazine*, writes for several newsletters and blogs, and gives workshops on short story writing and promotion. Kaye lives in Knoxville, Tennessee.

DARYL WOOD GERBER
darylwoodgerber.com

Daryl writes the nationally bestselling Cookbook Nook Mystery series. As Avery Aames, she pens the Agatha Award–winning, nationally bestselling Cheese Shop Mystery series. Daryl's short stories have been nominated for the Agatha, Anthony, and other awards. Fun tidbit: As an actress, Daryl appeared in *Murder, She Wrote.* Check out recipes on her blog at mysteryloverskitchen.com and friend her on Facebook.

BARB GOFFMAN
barbgoffman.com

Barb is the author of *Don't Get Mad, Get Even*, a collection of short stories published in 2013 by Wildside Press. She won the 2013 Macavity Award for Best Mystery Short Story, and she's been nominated ten times for national writing awards (the Agatha, Anthony, and Macavity Awards and the Pushcart Prize). Barb is a coordinating editor of the Chesapeake Crimes anthology series, serves as program chair of the Malice Domestic mystery convention, and recently opened a freelance editing service (goffmanediting.com) focusing on crime fiction.

PATRICIA GUSSIN

Patricia is a physician and the bestselling author of six medical-psychological thrillers. She is also a cofounder of Oceanview Publishing and serves as president and editor. She lives on Longboat Key, Florida, and in Amagansett, New York. Patricia and her husband, Bob, also a doctor and an author, are the proud owners of Oceanview Vineyards, located in Marlborough, New Zealand, associated with Villa Maria Estates Winery. Favorite tagline: From medicine and medical research to books and wine, heading in the right direction.

J. A. HENNRIKUS

J. A. Hennrikus has published three short stories with Level Best Books. She is the 2014 president of Sisters in Crime New England, serves on the national board of SinC, and belongs to Mystery Writers of America. She blogs at wickedcozyauthors.com. She also is the executive director of StageSource, a service organization for the New England theater community, and teaches classes in arts management at Emerson College. In 2015, she will debut the Clock Shop Mystery series under the name Julianne Holmes. Julie tweets as @JulieHennrikus.

NAOMI HIRAHARA

naomihirahara.com

Naomi is the Edgar Award–winning author of the Mas Arai mystery series, as well as a new series featuring a young, multiracial, female bicycle cop with the Los Angeles Police

Department. *Murder on Bamboo Lane: An Officer Ellie Rush Mystery* made its debut in April 2014. A former newspaper journalist, Naomi also writes nonfiction books, middle-grade fiction, and short stories.

NORMA HUSS

normahuss.com

Norma joined the Guppies in 1997, before she and many others had Internet access. She still has the snail-mail newsletter she received. Since her first full-length mystery was published a month before her eightieth birthday, she calls herself the Grandma Moses of Mystery. Although she lives in Pennsylvania, she sets her mysteries near Chesapeake Bay, inspired by the years she and her husband sailed there and beyond. As a grandma of eight, her newest book is for the grandchildren: *Cherish*, a YA ghost mystery.

ROBERTA ISLEIB

Roberta's twelfth mystery, *Murder with Ganache*, written as Lucy Burdette, was published in February 2014 by NAL. Her books and stories have been short-listed for Agatha, Anthony, and Macavity Awards. She is a past president of Sisters in Crime.

POLLY IYER

Polly is the author of six suspense novels: *Hooked, InSight, Murder Déjà Vu, Threads,* and two books—soon to be joined by a third—in the Diana Racine Psychic Suspense series, *Mind Games* and *Goddess of the Moon*. Born in a coastal city north of Boston, she now makes her home in beautiful upstate South Carolina.

TAMMY KAEHLER

tammykaehler.com

Tammy's career in marketing and technical writing landed her in the world of automobile racing, which inspired her with its blend of drama, competition, and friendly people. Mystery fans and racing insiders alike praised the first two Kate Reilly Racing Mysteries, *Dead Man's Switch* and *Braking Points*, and she takes readers behind the wheel for the third time in *Avoidable Contact*. Tammy works as a technical writer in the Los Angeles area, where she lives with her husband and many cars.

LAURIE R. KING

Laurie is a third-generation Northern Californian. Her twenty-two bestselling novels include twelve in the Mary Russell–Sherlock Holmes historical series, five in the contemporary Kate Martinelli series, several stand-alone novels, and now two Stuyvesant & Grey stories set in 1920s Europe. She has won the Edgar, Creasey, Lambda, Wolfe, and Macavity awards; been the guest of honor at Left Coast Crime, Bouchercon, and Malice Domestic; has an honorary doctorate from her graduate school; and was inducted into the Baker Street Irregulars. And yet she manages to spill coffee over her work as often as anyone else.

HARLEY JANE KOZAK

Harley's *Dating Dead Men* won the Agatha, Anthony, and Macavity Awards, and was followed by *Dating Is Murder*, *Dead Ex*, and *A Date You Can't Refuse*. Her short prose has appeared in *Ms. Magazine*, *The Sun*, *The Santa Monica Review*, and the anthologies *Mystery Muses*, *This Is Chick Lit*, *A Hell of a Woman*, *Butcher Knives and Body Counts*, *The Rich and the Dead*, and *Crimes by Moonlight*. She's an International Thriller Writers Award nominee, and her latest novel is the paranormal *Keeper of the Moon*. A sometimes actress, Harley lives with her kids and dogs in Southern California.

DEBORAH J LEDFORD

deborahjledford.com

Deborah's latest novel, *Crescendo*, is book three of the Steven Hawk/Inola Walela thriller series from Second Wind Publishing. In addition to a paperback and e-book, it is also available as an audiobook, narrated by Christina Cox (*Elysium*, *Chronicles of Riddick*, *Dexter*, *NCIS*, *24*), and produced by her media company, IOF Productions Ltd. Deborah's other novels include *Staccato* and *Snare*, the latter a Hillerman Sky Award and New Mexico–Arizona Book Awards finalist. She is a member of International Thriller Writers, Mystery Writers of America, and Sisters in Crime, and served as president of the SinC Desert Sleuths Chapter in 2012–2013.

KYLIE LOGAN

Kylie is the author of the League of Literary Ladies mysteries, the Chili Cook-Off mysteries, and the Ethnic Eats mysteries, all published by Berkley Prime Crime. As Casey Daniels, she is also the author of the Pepper Martin mysteries. Kylie has a degree in English and experience as a journalist and writing instructor. She began her career writing romance, and her book *Devil's Diamond* was nominated for a Romance Writers of America RITA Award for Best Historical Romance. She lives in northeast Ohio.

ALICE LOWEECEY

Baker of brownies and tormentor of characters, Alice recently celebrated her thirtieth year outside the convent. Her first three books starring ex-nun private investigator Giulia Falcone are *Force of Habit*, *Back in the Habit*, and *Veiled Threat*. Giulia will begin investigating again in January 2015 with new mysteries from Henery Press.

GAIL LUKASIK

gaillukasik.com

Gail writes the Leigh Girard mystery series. *Kirkus Reviews* said of *Death's Door*: "Lukasik's second...is fast-paced and literate, with a strong protagonist and a puzzle that keeps you guessing." *Peak Season for Murder*, the third book in her series, won a 2014 LOVEY Award for Best Traditional/Amateur Sleuth at the Love Is Murder Mystery Conference in Chicago. Gail began her writing career as a poet. Her most recent book of poems is *Homeless, in My Own Words: True Stories of Homeless Mothers*.

MARGARET MARON

margaretmaron.com

Margaret has written twenty-nine novels and two collections of short stories. Winner of the Edgar, Agatha, Anthony, and Macavity, her works are on the reading lists of various courses in contemporary Southern literature. She has served as president of Sisters in Crime, the American Crime Writers League, and Mystery Writers of America, which named her Grand Master in 2013. In 2008, she received the North Carolina Award, the state's highest civilian honor.

NANCY MARTIN

Nancy is the author of nearly fifty popular novels in four genres—mystery, romance, historical, and suspense. She is the author of the bestselling and award-winning Blackbird Sisters Mystery Series and the winner of the 2009 *RT* Career Achievement Award for Mystery/Suspense/Thriller. She is a founding member of Pennwriters and has served on the board of Sisters in Crime. Find her at facebook.com/authornancymartin.

SUJATA MASSEY

Sujata is the author of the Rei Shimura mystery series and the Daughters of Bengal historic espionage novels.

EDITH MAXWELL

A former organic farmer, Edith writes the Local Foods Mysteries, with organic farmer Cam Flaherty, the Locavore

Club, and locally sourced murder (Kensington Publishing). As Tace Baker, she writes the Speaking of Mystery series, featuring Quaker linguistics professor Lauren Rousseau (Barking Rain Press). Edith holds a PhD in linguistics and is a member of Amesbury Meeting of Friends. She also writes award-winning short crime fiction, belongs to Mystery Writers of America's New England Chapter, and is the secretary of Sisters in Crime's New England Chapter. A mother, technical writer, and fourth-generation Californian, she lives north of Boston in an antique house with her beau and three cats.

CATRIONA MCPHERSON

catrionamcpherson.com

Catriona is the Agatha, Lefty, and Macavity award-winning author of the Dandy Gilver series, set in Scotland in the 1920s, where (but not when) she was born. In 2013, she began a strand of modern, stand-alone suspense novels with the Lefty-nominated *As She Left It*. One of four sisters in life, she took to SinC with gusto upon moving to the United States in 2010 and is currently the vice president. Find her on Facebook, Twitter, Femmes Fatales, and Criminal Minds. If you're a stalker, find her in Northern California, where she lives with two black cats and a scientist.

JENNY MILCHMAN

Jenny is a suspense writer whose debut novel, *Cover of Snow*, was published in 2013 and won the Mary Higgins Clark Award. Her second novel, *Ruin Falls*, came out in April 2014, and her short fiction appears in *Ellery Queen Mystery Magazine* and the anthology *Adirondack Mysteries and Other Mountain Tales, Volume 2*. Jenny chairs the International Thriller Writers' Debut Authors Program and is the founder of Take Your Child to a Bookstore Day. She used to live with her family on the road on the world's longest book tour but recently settled in upstate New York. For now.

LIZ MUGAVERO

Liz is the author of the Pawsitively Organic Mysteries. The first book in the series, *Kneading to Die*, was an Agatha Award nominee for Best First Novel. As you can imagine, her canine and feline rescues demand the best organic food and treats around. She holds a BA in English from Salem State College and an MA in writing and publishing from Emerson College. She is a member of Sisters in Crime, Sisters in Crime New England, Mystery Writers of America, and the Cat Writers' Association.

CARLA NEGGERS

Carla started writing when she climbed a tree with pen and paper in hand at age eleven. Now she is a *New York Times* bestselling author of many novels of romantic suspense and contemporary romance, including *Cider Brook*, *Declan's Cross*, *Heron's Cove*, *Saint's Gate*, *That Night on Thistle Lane*, and *Secrets of the Lost Summer*. An avid traveler, Carla is always plotting her next adventure—whether in life or for one of her novels. She lives with her family on a hilltop in Vermont, near Quechee Gorge, where she is at work on her next novel.

CLARE O'DONOHUE

Clare is the author of seven novels in two series, the Someday Quilts Mysteries and the Kate Conway Mysteries. In addition, she has written two e-novellas and numerous magazine articles. She's the president of the Midwest Chapter of Mystery Writers of America and an active member of Sisters in Crime. She works as a television writer and producer, and lives near Chicago.

SUSAN OLEKSIW

Susan writes the Mellingham series, featuring Chief of Police Joe Silva (*Last Call for Justice*, 2012) and the Anita Ray series, featuring an Indian American photographer living at her aunt's tourist hotel in South India (*Under the Eye of Kali*, 2010). Susan is well known for her articles on crime fiction; her first publication on crime fiction was *A Reader's Guide to the Classic British Mystery*. Her short stories have appeared in *Alfred Hitchcock Mystery Magazine* and numerous anthologies. Her most recent publication is *For the Love of Parvati: An Anita Ray Mystery* (2014).

GIGI PANDIAN
gigipandian.com

Gigi is the *USA Today* bestselling author of the Jaya Jones Treasure Hunt Mystery Series. Her debut mystery novel, *Artifact*, was awarded a William F. Deeck–Malice Domestic Grant and was named a Best of 2012 debut novel by *Suspense Magazine*. Gigi spent her childhood being dragged around the world by her anthropologist parents and now lives in the San Francisco Bay Area.

SANDRA PARSHALL

Sandra is the author of the Agatha Award–winning Rachel Goddard mysteries. A former Chapter Liaison on the SinC board of directors, she also supervised the SinC discussion list for seven years and is a former member of the Chesapeake Chapter board. She lives in Northern Virginia.

CATHY PICKENS

Cathy's *Southern Fried* won the St. Martin's Press/Malice Domestic Best First Traditional Mystery Novel Competition. Featuring attorney Avery Andrews, it was called an "assured debut, a cozy with some sharp edges" by *Publishers Weekly* and was one of five finalists for *RT BOOKclub Magazine*'s 2004 award for best mystery. She has also written a mystery tour of Charleston, *Charleston Mysteries*, and writes a column on historic crime for *Mystery Readers Journal*. In her other life, Cathy is a lawyer and business professor at Queens University of Charlotte. She teaches MBA courses and workshops on developing the creative process.

LINDA RODRIGUEZ

Linda's *Every Broken Trust* was a selection of Las Comadres National Latino Book Club. Her first novel, *Every Last Secret*, won the St. Martin's Press/Malice Domestic Best First Traditional Mystery Novel Competition, was a Barnes & Noble mystery pick and a finalist for the International Latino Book Award. Her third Skeet Bannion mystery, *Every Hidden Fear*, will be published in May 2014. For her books of poetry, Linda has received numerous awards, including the Thorpe Menn Literary Excellence Award, Midwestern Voices and Visions Award, Elvira Cordero Cisneros Award, ArtsKC Fund Inspiration Award, and Ragdale and Macondo Fellowships.

CHRIS ROERDEN
writersinfo.info

Chris's fifty-year career as an editor includes workshop leader, university writing instructor, and author of *Don't Murder Your Mystery* (Agatha Award winner, Anthony and Macavity finalist, Writer's Digest Book Club selection) and its all-genre version, *Don't Sabotage Your Submission* (Benjamin Franklin Award winner, Florida Writers Royal Palm Book of the Year, *ForeWord Review* Writing Book of the Year finalist). Chris also wrote six books for clients and two books and a game as a volunteer. Currently she coordinates SinC's online list of "Reference Books for Writers by Sisters in Crime Members."

BARBARA ROSS

Barbara's novel *Clammed Up*, the first in her Maine Clambake Mystery series, was published by Kensington in September 2013. *Boiled Over* will come in May 2014. Barbara is a past president of Sisters in Crime New England and a coeditor and copublisher at Level Best Books, which publishes the anthology *Best New England Crime Stories* every November. Prior to turning to writing full time, Barbara was a cofounder and chief operating officer at WebCT. She and her husband live in Somerville, Massachusetts, and Boothbay Harbor, Maine.

LORI ROY

Lori's debut novel, *Bent Road*, won the Edgar Award for Best First Novel by an American Author and was named a 2011 *New York Times* Notable Crime Book and a 2012 notable book by the state of Kansas. *Bent Road* has been optioned for film by Cross Creek, with Mark Mallouk to adapt and Benderspink to produce. Her second novel, *Until She Comes Home*, was recently named a *New York Times* Editors' Choice. Lori also serves as treasurer for Sisters in Crime and is a liaison to the Author Coalition.

TERRY SHAMES

terryshames.com

Terry grew up in Texas and is the bestselling author of the Samuel Craddock mystery novels *A Killing at Cotton Hill* and *The Last Death of Jack Harbin*, set in the fictional town of Jarrett Creek, Texas. A resident of Berkeley, California, Terry is a board member of the Northern California chapters of Sisters in Crime and Mystery Writers of America.

JUNE SHAW

June is serving her third term representing Louisiana on the board of Mystery Writers of America's Southwest Chapter. Since a romantic interest plays an important role in her mysteries and she's also written a romance, she additionally serves as the Published Author Liaison for Southern Louisiana's chapter of Romance Writers of America. June writes in a variety of genres— with mystery at the forefront—and has been nominated for the David Award, given out by Deadly Ink Press for the best mystery of the year, and received favorable reviews from *Publishers Weekly*, *Kirkus Reviews*, bestselling authors, and other readers.

CLEA SIMON

cleasimon.com

Clea is the author of fifteen mysteries in the Theda Krakow, Dulcie Schwartz, and Pru Marlowe pet noir series. The latter two are ongoing and include her most recent books, *Grey Howl* (Severn House) and *Panthers Play for Keeps* (Poisoned Pen Press). A former journalist and nonfiction author, she lives in Somerville, Massachusetts, with her husband, the writer Jon Garelick, and their cat, Musetta.

PATRICIA SMILEY

patriciasmiley.com

Patricia's Tucker Sinclair novels have made several bestseller lists, including the *Los Angeles Times* list. Her short fiction has appeared in *Ellery Queen Mystery Magazine* and *Two of the Deadliest*, edited by Elizabeth George. Patty has served on the faculty of various writers' conferences, including the Surrey International Writers' Conference in British Columbia, the Jackson Hole Writers Conference in Wyoming, and Book Passage Mystery Writers Conference in Corte Madera, California. She served as vice president of the Southern California Chapter of Mystery Writers of America and as president of the Los Angeles Chapter of Sisters in Crime.

PATRICIA SPRINKLE

patriciasprinkle.com

A past president of SinC, Patricia lives in Georgia but grew up in North Carolina and Jacksonville. Her Southern roots are evident in twenty mysteries and four general novels that depict both Southern cities and small towns. Her novel *Hold Up the Sky* (2010) was a Southern Independent Booksellers OKRA pick. In her latest novel, *Friday's Daughter*, a young woman has to create a new life for herself when her dreams are dashed. When not writing, Patricia likes to read, snorkel, and work with growing plants and growing children.

ROCHELLE STAAB

rochellestaab.com

A former award-winning radio and music executive, Rochelle blends her love for mystery and a fascination with the supernatural in the bestselling Mind for Murder Mystery series. The witty whodunits partner Los Angeles psychologist Liz Cooper with religious philosophy professor Nick Garfield to investigate murders shadowed by an occult twist. The series' debut, *Who Do, Voodoo?*, earned Agatha, Anthony, and Eureka Best First Novel nominations. The follow-up, *Bruja Brouhaha*, won the Left Coast Crime 2013 Watson Award. Rochelle's latest novel, *Hex on the Ex*, is available now. Contact Rochelle on Facebook and Twitter, and on her website.

KELLI STANLEY
kellistanley.com

Kelli's work has won the Macavity, Golden Nugget, and Bruce Alexander Memorial Historical Mystery Awards, and has been nominated for the Shamus and the *Los Angeles Times* Book Prize. She is best known for the Miranda Corbie series (*City of Dragons, City of Secrets*), set in 1940s San Francisco and featuring a PI described by *Library Journal* as "one of crime's most arresting heroines." Kelli also writes a "Roman noir" series set in Roman Britain (*Nox Dormienda*). She lives in San Francisco and holds a Master's degree in Classics. *City of Ghosts*, her next novel, launches in August.

DIANE VALLERE
dianevallere.com

Diane is living proof that you can redesign your life with a little know-how and a lot of determination. After close to two decades working for a top luxury retailer, she traded fashion accessories for accessories to murder, now juggling four different mystery series: the Style & Error series, the Mad for Mod series, the Material Witness series and the upcoming Costume Shop series. Diane started her own detective agency at age ten and has maintained a passion for shoes, clues, and clothes ever since.

ELAINE VIETS
elaineviets.com

Elaine has written twenty-two novels in two series. Her bestselling Dead-End Job series is a satiric look at a serious subject, the minimum-wage world. Her character, Helen

Hawthorne, works a different low-paying job each book. Her latest Dead-End Job hardcover is *Catnapped!* Elaine's second series features mystery shopper Josie Marcus. Elaine won the Agatha, Anthony, and Lefty Awards. She is a member of the Chesapeake Chapter of Sisters in Crime and of MWA.

SHARON WILDWIND
wildwindauthor.com

Sharon is a Calgary, Alberta, mystery writer. She has one completed mystery series, featuring four returning Vietnam veterans. For these veterans, returning to civilian life is murder. She's currently at work on a stand-alone novel, set in modern-day Calgary. She tweets as @sharww.

ABOUT THE EDITORS

HANK PHILLIPPI RYAN

hankphillippiryan.com

Hank is the on-air investigative reporter for Boston's NBC affiliate. She has won thirty-two Emmys, twelve Edward R. Murrow Awards, and dozens of other honors for her groundbreaking journalism. A bestselling author of six mystery novels, Hank has won multiple prestigious awards for her crime fiction: three Agathas, the Anthony, Macavity, and Daphne, and, for *The Other Woman*, the coveted Mary Higgins Clark Award. National reviews have called her a "master at crafting suspenseful mysteries" and "a superb and gifted storyteller." Her mystery-thriller *The Wrong Girl* won the 2014 Agatha Award for Best Contemporary Novel and the 2014 Daphne Award for Best Mainstream Suspense. A six-week *Boston Globe* bestseller, it was dubbed "another winner" in a *Booklist* starred review. *Truth Be Told*, next in the series from Forge Books, is coming October 2014. Hank is a founding teacher at Mystery Writers of America University and was 2013 president of Sisters in Crime.

ELAINE WILL SPARBER

elainewillsparber.com

Elaine is a writer and editor from Long Island, New York. Her short story "Cover Story" is included in *Fish Nets: The Second Guppy Anthology*, published by Wildside Press in 2013. She has also coauthored a travel book and ghostwritten two health books. In 2003, after working as a staff editor for several book publishers for twenty-three years, Elaine became an independent editor, founding the Sharp Pencil Editorial Services.